NEW DIRECTIONS FOR INSTITUTIONAL RESEARCH

Patrick T. Terenzini
The Pennsylvania State University
EDITOR-IN-CHIEF

Ellen Earle Chaffee
North Dakota Board of Higher Education
ASSOCIATE EDITOR

Total Quality Management in Higher Education

Lawrence A. Sherr
The University of Kansas

Deborah J. Teeter
The University of Kansas

EDITORS

Number 71, Fall 1991

JOSSEY-BASS INC., PUBLISHERS, San Francisco

MAXWELL MACMILLAN INTERNATIONAL PUBLISHING GROUP
New York • Oxford • Singapore • Sydney • Toronto

TOTAL QUALITY MANAGEMENT IN HIGHER EDUCATION
Lawrence A. Sherr, Deborah J. Teeter (eds.)
New Directions for Institutional Research, no. 71
Volume XVIII, Number 3
Patrick T. Terenzini, Editor-in-Chief
Ellen Earle Chaffee, Associate Editor

Microfilm copies of issues and articles are available in 16mm and 35mm, as well as microfiche in 105mm, through University Microfilms Inc., 300 North Zeeb Road, Ann Arbor, Michigan 48106.

LC 85-645339   ISSN 0271-0579   ISBN 1-55542-773-1

NEW DIRECTIONS FOR INSTITUTIONAL RESEARCH is part of The Jossey-Bass Adult and Higher Education Series and is published quarterly by Jossey-Bass Inc., Publishers, 350 Sansome Street, San Francisco, California 94104-1310 (publication number USPS 098-830). Second-class postage paid at San Francisco, California, and at additional mailing offices. POSTMASTER: Send address changes to New Directions for Institutional Research, Jossey-Bass Inc., Publishers, 350 Sansome Street, San Francisco, California 94104-1310.

SUBSCRIPTIONS for 1991 cost $45.00 for individuals and $60.00 for institutions, agencies, and libraries.

EDITORIAL CORRESPONDENCE should be sent to the Editor-in-Chief, Patrick T. Terenzini, Center for the Study of Higher Education, The Pennsylvania State University, 403 South Allen Street, Suite 104, University Park, Pennsylvania 16801-5202.

Photograph of the library by Michael Graves at San Juan Capistrano by Chad Slattery © 1984. All rights reserved.

Printed on acid-free paper in the United States of America.

THE ASSOCIATION FOR INSTITUTIONAL RESEARCH was created in 1966 to benefit, assist, and advance research leading to improved understanding, planning, and operation of institutions of higher education. Publication policy is set by its Publications Board.

For information about the Association for Institutional Research, write to:

AIR Executive Office
314 Stone Building
Florida State University
Tallahassee, FL 32306-3038

(904) 644-4470

CONTENTS

INTRODUCTION

You can't get the business office to bend a policy, yet the student's request makes more sense than the policy. Your credit card bill arrives four weeks before you expect to see your travel reimbursement check. You don't know whether anyone reads your report, but you have to write it anyway. Your admissions staff and your faculty blame each other while enrollment continues to slide.

I first began to notice problems like these in my university over twenty years ago. I decided to try harder not only to find solutions myself but also to persuade others to make changes. I even tried a few power plays. For seven years, nothing really worked.

Frustrated, I went back to graduate school for three years of intensive organizational studies. Then I went on to five years in full-time organizational research, which consisted for the most part of fieldwork on diverse campuses. Finally, eager to see whether I could now practice what I had learned, I returned to administration six years ago. And although all those lessons stood me in good stead, I also learned something new: One person (even a team of like-minded people) can have only a limited effect. I also learned that the world is always throwing us a new curveball for which research is important but not completely adequate preparation.

A fortuitous invitation arrived three years ago. The National Center for Postsecondary Governance and Finance suggested that I write an article synthesizing organizational measures that can be taken to improve academic quality. Maybe if I could integrate my research with my experience, the article would rally more like-minded people to work together according to good management principles and toward a common vision.

I struggled. I rewrote the article four times. Most of the key ideas were there, but it just wasn't coming together. As the deadline approached, fate intervened. Deborah Teeter introduced me to Lawrence Sherr, and he introduced me to Total Quality Management (TQM). The article became my first attempt to describe how TQM might work in the academic setting.

The TQM framework organized my fledgling ideas. It revealed and filled the gaps in my thinking. It resolved a great mystery left by my research: Why did college administrators, tackling an organizational problem, persist in doing what their business faculty, the Management 101 textbooks, and even their own common sense could have told them was the wrong thing to do? Now I know why, and I know how to change it. You will, too, when you understand TQM.

Chapter One introduces the principles of Total Quality Management and is followed by two case studies of institutions implementing TQM: Delaware County Community College in Chapter Two and Oregon State

University in Chapter Three. Chapter Four discusses how assessment fits with TQM; Chapters Five and Six tackle cultural and leadership issues, respectively. The concluding chapter describes a key role institutional researchers and planners can play in implementing TQM.

After you have read this volume, I urge you to read books from the bibliography in Appendix B. Start a book club with your colleagues, and let the book club become an action team. The revolution has begun, and our future depends on its success.

Ellen Earle Chaffee
Series Associate Editor

Ellen Earle Chaffee is vice-chancellor for academic affairs of the North Dakota University System.

We can improve our management of higher education by
emphasizing our values regarding the importance of people,
knowledge, and continuous improvement.

Total Quality Management in Higher Education

Lawrence A. Sherr, G. Gregory Lozier

Adopting management concepts and practices developed in the business world is not new to higher education. Examples include the establishment of multiple levels of management (supervision) and a formal chain of command; the generation of many forms, reports, and data, many of which go unused; the implementation of multiple checks and approvals (inspections); the use of elaborate formal evaluations that frequently have no constructive basis; the encouragement of competitive bidding that often results in inexpensive (not to say cheap) materials but frequently increases total costs; and the institution of elaborate planning systems that often do not work well in setting direction, allocating resources, or both. These practices have been largely unsuccessful in achieving their designed objectives in the corporate world and are some of the reasons why many U.S. businesses are not competing adequately in today's global economy.

An alternative to many of these management practices is Total Quality Management (TQM). TQM is a style of management that has worked for several decades overseas and is receiving growing attention in the United States. Now some colleges and universities are beginning to recognize that TQM values are more compatible with higher education than many existing management systems. To understand what TQM has to offer higher education, you must first understand how TQM applies concepts of control, quality, process, and customer to management.

On first hearing, Total Quality Management is not a term that is easily embraced. The phrase *total quality* comes from "total quality control," originally coined by Feigenbaum (1983). All of us in higher education want the services we provide to be of the highest quality, but we are much less likely to agree about how to define and measure that quality. Furthermore, both the words *control* and *management* suggest centralization and authoritarianism, so they typically elicit resounding displeasure on the college or university campus. Yet total quality control relates not to managerial decision making but to statistical control (Shewhart, 1931), and the need to develop processes that are stable and predictable. If we are to accept the notion of controlled processes, in contrast to controlled personnel, we are more likely to put aside our biases in order to understand what TQM is and what it can mean for higher education.

The Language of TQM

Consumers describe quality by the characteristics of the product or service they acquire: It works, it is durable, it is available, service is good, and employees are courteous. In this consumer-oriented context, the quality of a service or product has three dimensions: its design, output, and process. *Design* refers to the intended characteristics of the output. The design should reflect consumer need, and it includes the specifications of the output, the scope of the product or service, the time frame for delivery, and the supplies, materials, and human resources needed to develop the output. *Output,* on the other hand, refers to the actual product or service; it represents what the consumer actually receives. Such matters as structure and durability are related to the output, which typically has measurable elements. From the consumer's point of view, the quality of the design and the quality of the output can be quite different things. Today, for example, a slide rule might be of high quality in terms of output, but it will not sell well because such computational technology as the electronic calculator offers higher quality in terms of design.

In the framework of TQM, *process*—or the flow of work activities—is the most critical dimension of quality. The process includes the determination of who the real customer is and whom to involve in the design. Plotting the process in a flowchart (one of the basic TQM tools) identifies the various stages of design and output production. The quality of the process often receives little attention when managers or administrators want to change a product or service. Instead, there are several typical ways that managers deal with process: Sometimes mistakes are made in one aspect of a larger process, such as registration, payroll, or even teaching. The term for fixing earlier mistakes is *rework.* Or perhaps administrators decide to throw away the work that has been done and start over again; in other words, they decide to *scrap* the work. Finally, most processes include steps that do not add value and thereby cause *unnecessary complexity.* A major goal of TQM is to eliminate scrap, rework, and unnecessary complexity.

Because of the paramount role of processes in the quality of a product or service, we will focus this examination of Total Quality Management on process. Examples of processes in higher education that could benefit from immediate application of TQM principles are provided, and additional concepts are discussed.

A Process Examined: A Brief Case Study

Administrators on both the academic and nonacademic sides of a large state university determined that the new-appointment payroll process was not working well, as errors and complaints were common. All participants blamed everyone but themselves for the mistakes. The payroll office blamed the departments and employees who initiated the forms for not providing accurate or complete information. The individuals who initiated the forms blamed the payroll office for entering information incorrectly and for not processing new appointments in a timely fashion. A preliminary analysis revealed that 50 percent of the forms were either incompletely or incorrectly filled out. This is not surprising, given that there was no required training program for those completing the form. Ninety percent of the problems were typically corrected by making a telephone call—that is, by rework. The remaining 10 percent of the incorrect forms were sent back to the departments to reinitiate the process; in other words, they were scrapped.

Using statistical control methodologies, Total Quality Management provides systematic tools for examining any process. Appendix A provides a synopsis of some of these tools. In the example at hand, analysts constructed a flowchart of the process, which demonstrated that, depending on where in the organization the transaction began, the new-appointment payroll process required from three to seven inspections, or signatures. A Pareto chart (see Appendix A) of the frequency of different types of mistakes revealed that about half of the transactions involved student help and that these transactions accounted for 70 percent of the errors.

The analysis suggested that many of the inspections were adding considerable cost to the process but were not adding corresponding value. After much debate, authorities experimentally eliminated inspections, and despite the fears of some that the error rate would increase, the number of mistakes actually declined. Moreover, the time taken for an appointment form to reach the payroll office was reduced by forty-eight hours.

This example has another chapter. State employment policy requires that every new classified employee attend an orientation program within twenty-one days of employment. But orientation for new employees at this university rarely occurred within that time period. Further analysis of the process flowcharts revealed that the personnel department, which scheduled the orientations, did not hear about a new hire until after the appointment forms had cleared the payroll office. Data revealed that on average the personnel department received the form seventeen days after the employee was hired, with a standard deviation of eleven. The first proposed solution was to make the process even more complex by adding another copy to the form. But at this point in the analysis, a change in personnel introduced an individual unfamiliar with the problem and not yet committed to the TQM approach for improving the process. At present, without that commitment from the leadership, process refinement has stalled. As a result, such issues as the student error rate, the need for training for individuals completing the form, and the need for timely orientation programs have not been satisfactorily addressed yet.

In 1987 the U.S. established the Malcolm Baldrige National Quality Award. The "Finding and Purposes" section states that "American business and industry are beginning to understand that poor quality costs companies as much as 20 percent of sales revenues nationally" (Public Law 100-107). The example just described demonstrates that rework, scrap, and unnecessary complexity add cost to and lower the quality of a product or service. It also illustrates how analyzing data generated by the process itself can yield obvious steps for process improvement.

Continuous Process Improvement

Ellen Earle Chaffee has observed that "quality is a verb, not a noun" (personal communication). As such, TQM is not a passive descriptive term but an energetic activity—that of continuous process improvement. The five key ingredients for continuous process improvement are honesty, shared vision, patience, commitment, and TQM theory. Only the TQM theory can be taught and learned. The remaining ingredients require a different type of personal and organizational commitment.

Honesty. Solving a problem requires admitting that it exists. Thus, improving a process requires first acknowledging that there is room for improvement. The popular media broadcast many examples of problems in contemporary higher education, among them the poor academic preparation of entering students, racism, sexism, cheating, poor advising, the poor quality of student life, the excessive expansion of administrative and support services personnel, and costs that are escalating at a rate far exceeding inflation. When higher education itself contributes to one of these problems—and especially when it is solely responsible—then it can and must do something. After acknowledging the problem, the critical next step is to determine who has the power to improve the situation. Almost always, it is management.

Shared Vision. Continuous process improvement requires the participation of everyone involved. Support for total quality requires a shared vision that processes can be improved and that, in turn, similar improvements will be realized in design, output, and costs.

Patience. Raising the quality of our services through continuous process improvement takes study and time—a great deal of time. If a significant portion of an organization's resources is being used unwisely, targets for budget reduction or reallocation usually cannot be identified in a day. Hasty budget cutting often leads to lower-quality output. It is better to develop a budget process that uses the resources effectively in the first place so that budget cuts are less likely. There is no magic wand that can create such a process in an instant; patience is required.

Commitment. Equally important is commitment, for without it frustration is likely to overcome efforts at improvement in those moments when patience wanes. This commitment must come from all levels, including the president, other administrators, faculty, staff, students, and board members, if institution-wide process improvements are to be realized. However, no one office has to wait for the entire institution to "buy in" before beginning to implement TQM concepts or tools. Just as one college of a university might benefit from the use of an effective strategic planning process even if the entire university has not implemented it, so too an individual college or office can benefit from embracing TQM.

TQM Theory. As noted earlier, this is the only ingredient that can be learned from others. The following section outlines the theory of TQM.

An Introduction to TQM Theory

The theoretical foundations of Total Quality Management came from several people, including W. Edwards Deming, recognized internationally for enabling Japanese industrial systems to achieve their current worldwide reputation for quality. Deming's (1986) philosophy is captured in his "fourteen points for management." Individuals seeking a broad grounding in TQM should become familiar with these fourteen points. Other useful formulations include the work of Juran (1988, 1989), who also assisted the Japanese in the 1950s, and Crosby (1979), who developed his ideas at ITT.

For this introduction to the theory of TQM, we focus on five areas: mission and customer focus; systematic approach to operations; vigorous development of human resources; long-term thinking; and, again, commitment. These five points form a complete theoretical system, and one cannot fully understand any one point without the other four.

Mission and Customer Focus. Studies of success stories in industry reveal that virtually every successful company has a driving desire to focus on satisfying customer needs. These companies recognize that the most important part of any organization is the customer and that to capture and hold customers you must satisfy their needs. Satisfying the customer requires knowing first who the customer is. An organization's mission statement is usually a good source of customer identification. Yet because higher education is often loath to recognize the concept of customer, our mission statements rarely provide adequate clarification. Most college and university mission statements identify the services performed, such as teaching, research and scholarship, and community service. However, these statements seldom assist in determining which services are or are not appropriate in light of its customers. We are often more clear about what we do than for whom, and we attend better to our needs or to their needs as we see them than to their needs as *they* see them.

Derek Bok ("Debate over College Costs and Quality," 1990), speaking to Harvard's board of overseers in response to public criticism of higher education, said, "Most of the charges are flawed because they ignore basic conflicts and contradictions in the demands society makes on universities. By ignoring the conflicts that underlie so many of the complaints, the debate will remain superficial. . . . In particular, we need to step back and ask whether our universities are doing all they might to help the country address its most important problems—lagging competitiveness, poverty, inadequate public education, environmental hazards, and many more" (p. A2). This admonition by Bok is a call for customer focus—a call, in fact, to know our mission.

It is important to recognize that everyone in the organization is both a supplier and a customer. As a supplier you serve both external and internal customers; as an internal customer, you are served by other suppliers within the organization. If anyone does a bad job, the next person must either rework the task, send it back to have it done all over again, or, worse yet, pass it on to the next internal customer. Any of these actions typically results in increased costs and lower quality. Customer focus requires that we know who our internal customers are, whether we are satisfying their needs, and whether we can satisfy them better.

Knowing our mission and customers makes it feasible to measure performance against stated purposes. Measurement provides feedback and allows the organization to enact successive changes that improve the three dimensions of quality already discussed—design, process, and output. Such improvement requires persistence.

Systematic Approach to Operations. TQM requires systematic, not random, continuous improvement of the dimensions of quality. The Shewhart (1931) cycle—plan-do-check-act (PDCA)—offers a scientific method for continuous process improvement:

Plan: Identify a process in need of improvement, analyze the problems, and develop a proposal for change that will cause some type of improvement.
Do: Run an experiment with the proposed change.
Check: Collect data to determine if the experiment produced the desired change.
Act: If the experiment is successful, implement the idea more broadly; if not, learn from the mistake and try an alternative.

Knowledge and science are often advanced by rejecting hypotheses. Failures are just as important as victories if we learn from them. The PDCA cycle should be thought of as a continuous loop going from one proposal and experiment to the next.

The PDCA cycle applies to any process, including instruction. As we implied in the new-appointment payroll case study, every process generates the data necessary to improve it. Such data can be found in a grade book, for example. In one statistics class of 300 students, the relationship between homework submission and final exam performance had a 0.6 coefficient of determination. Although the professor presented this evidence during the introductory lectures of the course, many students continued not to complete homework. Teaching assistants (TAs) collected and graded homework, but they did not report delinquent homework assignments to the professor until the end of the semester. The case provided an opportunity to implement the PDCA cycle.

The class is a two-hour lecture with a ten-minute break. The proposed change was to have TAs report a homework count to the professor at the break. When counts were down, students were reminded of the homework-exam relationship and urged to do their assignments in the future. Although homework completion has not been 100 percent, homework submissions and exam performance have been higher since implementing the change in the process.

The goal of all organizations should be to make their processes both stable and predictable—in other words, in control. If internal and external customers can be assured that the output they receive has a minimum of variation, customers can improve their own processes. Any aspect of higher education—from the curriculum and advising to payroll, purchasing, and travel reimbursement—can benefit from predictable input. For example, consider teaching course B that has a prerequisite of course A. If the instructor can count on students knowing material from course A, it will be much easier to teach course B, and educational quality will be improved.

Vigorous Development of Human Resources. William Golomski, a quality improvement consultant and lecturer at the University of Chicago, has stated in conversation that managers deal with transactions, whereas leaders deal with the transformation of an organization. Continuous improvement of quality is also concerned with organizational transformation, but too few individuals in higher education participate in the ongoing personal and professional development that prepares them to improve processes. Department chairs, for example, often become chairs because they are excellent professors, but this does not guarantee that they can prepare a departmental budget or lead other professionals. Nevertheless, the college or university rarely provides formal training. Many teaching faculty initially entered the classroom with no formal education in pedagogy. We cannot expect employees who have never learned how to do a job to do a top-quality job.

A principal element in the area of human resource development is empowerment. Empowerment means that the employees closest to the impact of a decision have a critical role to play in the determination of that decision. The result—less management—has been described by Likins (1990), president of Lehigh University, as follows: "People at lower levels in the organization have more responsibility and more freedom to exercise it; the combination translates into more power. They need fewer approvals, so they have more autonomy in making decisions. They have to trust and respect each other more to get the job done, because there is less supervision and more reliance on cooperation."

Long-Term Thinking. Drucker (1974) describes it best: Long-term thinking is molding the future by understanding the consequences of what we do today. Long-term thinking requires a willingness to forgo short-term benefits that undermine future well-being. Such thinking is congruent with knowing our mission and focusing on our customers, with systematic improvement, and continuing human resource development. Every day we delay in beginning to improve processes, another day is wasted. Begin the journey today and serve as a model for others in your organization.

Commitment. Ensuring quality is not a spectator sport. It cannot be delegated to someone else. Everyone must become involved in improving and maintaining the quality of an institution.

Conclusion

If you think that these ideas make sense for industry but that higher education is different, be assured that many corporate leaders have responded in like fashion: "But we are different." Higher education *is* different, and our conservativeness does make it difficult. But consider the values that TQM espouses.

Importance of People. TQM reduces costs, but not in an authoritarian fashion. It has checks and balances. It empowers all the people involved and encourages less management control. Certainly valuing people is compatible with the philosophy and goals of higher education.

Need to Use Knowledge. It is surprising how faculty can become administrators and then not use what they know. For example, statisticians often do not use statistics, and scientists often do not use the scientific method. Also, most people in organizations know where problems lie in their own work processes. Let us all use our knowledge.

Continuous Improvement. What is education itself—our core mission—but continuous improvement through learning? Surely we want to endorse that idea as a description not only of our educational goal but also of our organizations as a whole.

We in higher education hold dearly such values as the importance of people, knowledge, and continuing improvement. Why don't we practice what we preach? If we do, over a long period of time—not next week, not next year, but over a five- to ten-year period—we will see significant improvements.

Institutional researchers can and should play a leading role in this transformation. The chapters that follow show how some institutions have begun the process of change. The final chapter suggests how institutional researchers might initiate TQM in their own operations and become model practitioners within their colleges and universities. There is no formula or list to follow; each institution must find the appropriate means for its unique culture. The stories that follow should stimulate your own thought.

References

Crosby, P. B. *Quality Is Free*. New York: McGraw-Hill, 1979.

"Debate over College Costs and Quality Masks Deeper Problems, Says Harvard's Bok." *Chronicle of Higher Education*, April 18, 1990, p. A2.

Deming, W. E. *Out of the Crisis*. Cambridge: Massachusetts Institute of Technology, Center for Advanced Engineering Study, 1986.

Drucker, P. F. *Management: Tasks, Responsibilities, Practices*. New York: Harper & Row, 1974.

Feigenbaum, A. V. *Total Quality Control*. (3rd ed.) New York: McGraw-Hill, 1983.

Juran, J. M. *Juran on Planning for Quality*. New York: Free Press, 1988.

Juran, J. M. *Juran on Leadership for Quality: An Executive Handbook*. New York: Free Press, 1989.

Likins, P. "In an Era of Tight Budgets and Public Criticism, Colleges Must Rethink Their Goals and Priorities." *Chronicle of Higher Education*, May 9, 1990, pp. B1–B2.

Public Law 100-107. Malcom Baldrige National Quality Award, 1987.

Shewhart, W. A. *Economic Control of Quality of Manufactured Product*. New York: Van Nostrand Reinhold, 1931.

Lawrence A. Sherr is Chancellors Club Teaching Professor and professor of business administration at The University of Kansas.

G. Gregory Lozier is executive director of planning and analysis at The Pennsylvania State University and is a member of the graduate faculty in higher education.

A community college implements Total Quality Management to conserve resources, improve effectiveness, capture the quality niche, and increase participation in decision making.

Total Quality Management Goes to Community College

Richard D. DeCosmo, Jerome S. Parker, Mary Ann Heverly

Higher education has always sought to improve itself. No one in higher education would admit wanting to maintain the current quality of programs and services—not because the quality is poor or mediocre but because it is somehow unacceptable not to be striving always for "excellence." This explains why educators constantly seek ways to manage their institutions better. But why should they choose Total Quality Management (TQM)? Simply put, the complex and difficult problems facing higher education in the nineties demand an entirely new approach to problem solving. Delaware County Community College (DCCC) chose TQM as its new problem-solving paradigm in the search for quality because we believe that it best addresses some of the challenges we will face in the last decade of the twentieth century.

The Challenges Ahead

Conserve Resources. For many years, solving problems or making improvements meant spending more money. Colleges added staff, built facilities, purchased equipment, enrolled more students, and temporarily made many problems less visible, even if they were not solved. They "papered over" their mistakes with money.

However, resources are not as plentiful as they once were; cost is a major issue for colleges as resistance to higher tuition levels builds and financial problems at the state and federal levels limit the funds available to colleges. Colleges must control costs and find reliable sources of additional revenue merely to keep resources from declining. Conservation of resources

New Directions for Institutional Research, no. 71, Fall 1991 © Jossey-Bass Inc., Publishers will be one of the more complex issues of the nineties. Many businesses now realize that eliminating waste, inefficiency, and rework (doing things over again) leads to improvements in processes and that this approach does not require new resources. The development of new programs and services necessary to survive in the nineties requires an economy and an "elegance" that higher education is not accustomed to achieving. The TQM paradigm offers tools and principles to control costs while improving quality.

Improve Effectiveness. Governments and the public are scrutinizing higher education more closely than ever before. They question the quality of higher education and demand greater accountability. Student retention is a serious problem for most colleges. The alarmingly low retention rate of minority students is an even more serious problem for society. More students need remedial assistance in order to succeed in college-level courses. For community colleges such as DCCC, the heterogeneity of the student body compounds the problem. Although many DCCC students can attend the college of their choice, DCCC is the only opportunity for higher education for others. If all students are to have the opportunity community colleges claim to give, these schools must achieve a level of effectiveness that few educational institutions have attained.

While most programs and services are of adequate quality today, DCCC believes that "good enough" is no longer good enough. The principles and methods embodied in Total Quality Management, especially its emphasis on continuous improvement, can provide an affordable avenue to excellent programs and services. Students have a right to expect nothing less.

Capture the Quality Niche. Competition increases as the number of traditional students declines, and prospective students enjoy a buyer's market. As customers, they want more and better services, especially as prices rise. Through the nineties competition will become more intense. Colleges that survive the competition will be those that best meet the requirements of their students and communities. Colleges that garner more resources will be those in which constituents and benefactors want to invest. Adopting TQM will give colleges the credibility they need to attract these investments. DCCC wants to capture the quality niche in order to meet the competition of the nineties.

Increase Participation in Decision Making. Although higher education claims to believe in collegiality, few colleges have an effective paradigm for encouraging participation in decision making. The complexity and immediacy of the problems and opportunities overwhelm even well-intentioned systems of governance. Solving today's problems requires the intelligence and hard work of everyone. TQM offers a paradigm that encourages effective participation. To achieve giant strides in both quality and efficiency, everyone must be freed to pursue quality and accept responsibility for it, to work together in teams, and to listen to internal and external customers.

The DCCC Plan

Implementing TQM in any organization constitutes a revolution in thinking and an evolution in practice. Because consistency and constancy of purpose are essential to such a change, the first step must be the education of the executive team. The DCCC executive team joined nine company teams that wanted to institute TQM in their organizations. These teams soon learned that the change required a paradigm shift, a culture change. The teams learned a new set of rules and tools for problem solving. In fact, the set of assumptions underlying the style of management required by this new paradigm differs from the assumptions underlying the current style of management in most organizations.

To begin applying TQM, an implementation team (I-team) took charge of planning, executing, and monitoring the transition process at DCCC. The I-team assigned one full-time staff member to work with team members. The team carefully chose a title, coordinator of TQ resources, that would prevent college staff from viewing the person occupying this position as solely responsible for implementation. The I-team then developed a three-part plan for the college.

Part I: Implement Total Quality in the Management of the College. The targeted time period for this part of the plan was 1986–1991. It had three overlapping phases. First, the I-team used several "waves" of project teams to initiate improvement projects and provide opportunities for training staff. Members across all functional units of the college comprised these teams. The teams focused on problems in the following areas: telephone service (in the admissions office), academic computing, assignment of students to curricula, staff parking, student employment, photocopying, and facilities usage. To support this effort, the college developed its own training program. The college obtained grants from corporate sponsors to acquire, review, and organize a library of training materials and to develop a curriculum for the program.

Encouraging administrative departments to implement TQM principles in their work characterized the second phase. All administrators experienced formal TQM training, research staff and a few others mastered the basic tools, and some staff acquired team-facilitator skills. All of these resources are now available to departments implementing TQM. Examples of areas the departments chose for improvement include class scheduling, services to off-campus centers, nursing student admissions, student entry, facilities usage, custodial and cleaning services, the hiring of part-time faculty, the budget process, work orders, purchase orders, and travel reimbursement.

Third, the executive team recognized the need to integrate all TQM efforts by using its tools in the college's planning process. This phase is occurring as we write this chapter. Planning, using TQM concepts, will become the most critical factor in the continuing efforts to infuse TQM throughout the organization.

The Self-Study for Reaccreditation. The results of DCCC's self-study for reaccreditation by the Middle States Association of Schools and Colleges will inform and support the planning process. The self-study approach, which was instituted in 1989–90, borrows heavily from TQM. The study cochairs as well as the chairs of the study's committees made a strong commitment to quality improvement at the onset of their work. The study itself focuses on the effectiveness of the general education component in all programs. During a four-week development program prior to the study, these important campus leaders, many of them faculty members, educated themselves about the self-study improvement process. They committed themselves to define carefully what they would study and improve, to collect data to determine the strengths and weaknesses of current efforts, and to analyze the data carefully in order to make recommendations for improving the college processes and systems that affect the achievement of general education competencies.

The assessment of general education competencies is proceeding in a deliberate, analytical manner and is meeting all the requirements of the Total Quality Management improvement process. We expect that self-study findings will lead to substantive improvements in the education of our students. This approach to conducting a self-study results in faculty and staff acquiring new knowledge about processes and systems that we thought we knew and understood.

Case Study of a Phase I DCCC Project Team. One of the college's first improvement projects shows how the application of TQM tools can make lasting improvements not only in a selected problem area but also in how staff seek improvements in their work areas. The Phone Project, as it came to be called, shows how rather simple problem-solving tools and group techniques, when applied in a disciplined fashion, can contribute to the ultimate success of any improvement effort. The project team, comprised of admissions staff who handle phone calls on a regular basis, used the plan-do-check-act (PDCA) improvement process (Deming, 1986; Walton, 1986) as a problem-solving framework.

The problem confronting the Phone Project team stemmed from a course registration system that encouraged nondegree students taking one or two courses to register by phone. The college had not anticipated the system's overwhelming effect on telephone operations. The purposes of phone registration are to ease registration for the large number of part-time students who find it difficult to register in person and to reduce the long lines and general mayhem associated with "field house" registration. However, phone registration created a new problem. Prospective students calling the admissions office for information, catalogues, or other purposes often could not complete their calls. A multiline phone console operated by the receptionist in the admissions office routed most calls. The result was a major bottleneck; callers experienced interminable busy signals or indefinite holds.

Before implementation of TQM and the PDCA cycle, the approach would have been to blame the receptionist (too slow, takes too many breaks) or to patch the system haphazardly by adding phone lines and staff during peak times (which often occur unpredictably). In fact, the team took the latter approach initially, but the situation appeared to deteriorate. The mistake lay in skipping the crucial planning phase. The team had arrived at solutions with limited data and little consultation with the staff who operate the system. Because team members did not have a data-rich problem definition, they had no reliable way to evaluate whether the solutions actually improved matters. No lasting improvement resulted from this first attempt at a solution.

After repeatedly applying the PDCA cycle, the team made significant, verifiable improvements. As a result of system changes made during the first PDCA cycle, the percent of lost or abandoned calls was reduced from 19 percent to 0 percent of incoming calls. The changes created enough slack in the system so that anyone trying to register or get information by phone could do so anytime during business hours. The improvements involved system changes, primarily the off-loading of certain kinds of calls to phone "hunt" groups, which allow calls to hunt automatically for the next open line without a central console. None of these changes required additional staff or phone lines.

The following outline of the Plan Phase illustrates the kinds of tools and techniques used by the team, describes what typically occurs during each phase of the PDCA cycle, and summarizes the activities of the Phone Project team.

Step 1: Define the problem in operational terms. Many people are unable to reach the admissions office without being put on hold.

Step 2: State the improvement objective in operational terms. To eliminate lost calls due to callers being put on hold by the admissions receptionist.

Step 3: Analyze the current situation. To better understand why callers could not get through and why calls were lost, the team brainstormed possible causes using a cause-and-effect diagram (see Figure 1 and the tool definitions in Appendix A). This is a useful problem-solving tool that graphically presents the relationship between problems or effects and their many sources or causes. It is sometimes called a "fishbone" diagram because of its resemblance to a fish skeleton.

Discussion of the cause-and-effect diagram led the team to believe that the distribution of calls was probably the greatest cause of the problem. The team then created a flowchart of incoming phone traffic (see Figure 2). First, they listed the kinds of calls that come into the admissions office and traced their routes. The resulting chart confirmed the suspected problem. Almost all incoming calls were routed through extension 5050, the admissions receptionist's phone console.

Figure 1. Telephone Project Cause-and-Effect Diagram

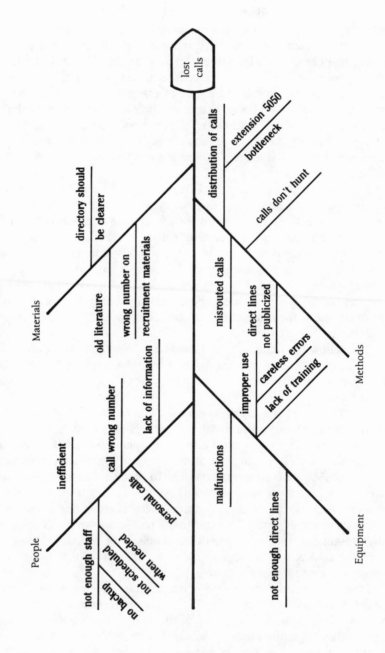

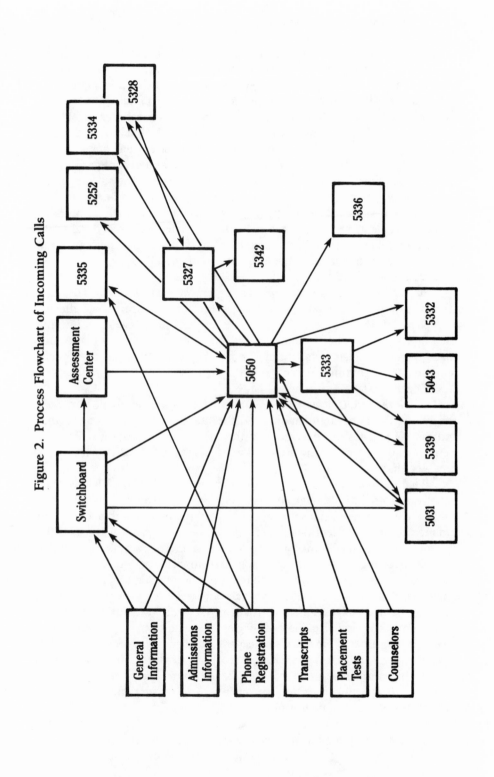

Figure 2. Process Flowchart of Incoming Calls

At this point the team felt confident that they had focused on the major problem area. To verify their opinion and to learn more about the nature of the problem, the team developed a data collection plan. They collected data to determine the types and frequency of calls, times when lines were full, level of hunt group activity, number of technical problems, adequacy of staffing coverage, and number of lost calls. Analysis of the data enabled the team to develop several improvement strategies. For instance, the team shifted phone registration calls to new and reconfigured hunt groups during the peak hours from 10:00 A.M. to 3:00 P.M. They also directed calls for advising and placement testing to another line. In addition, they took steps to standardize the processing of calls. Data analysis revealed frequent problems resulting from misrouting of calls and procedural problems when using various features such as call forwarding. The team dealt with these problems in subsequent iterations of the PDCA cycle.

Do Phase

Step 1: Develop a plan for implementing improvement strategies. The team developed a plan for making the changes and for measuring their effect.

Step 2: Follow the plan. The team met regularly to review its monitoring data and to make sure the implementation went according to plan. They made frequent adjustments, but most often they found that recurring problems stemmed from insufficient training.

Check Phase

Check the results against the objectives. The team carefully documented the timing of changes and monitored the number of lost calls and other indicators. These strategies reduced the percentage of lost calls from 19 percent to 0 percent during a month when registration was heaviest.

Act Phase

What did the team learn? Did the team meet its objectives? Is additional improvement needed? Although the team met the objective of eliminating lost calls, the team members soon realized that maintaining this condition required continuous identification of other refinements that would enable the system to handle an ever-increasing volume of calls. They also found that any process involving people cannot be expected to yield "zero defects" or zero lost calls, at least not on a constant basis, without persistent monitoring and adjusting. The team continues to cycle and recycle through the PDCA sequence. This involves almost constant revision of flowcharts and lists of causes and the piloting of new strategies. The latest strategy uses a voice messaging system to off-load calls requesting catalogues and course schedules. The receptionist diverts these calls to a recorded message unit so that names and mailing addresses can be retrieved from the unit during nonpeak times.

Part II: Develop a TQM Curriculum. The targeted time period for the second part of the plan was 1987–1991.

Curriculum development had two aspects: to develop a program for contracted training for businesses and other organizations and to offer a credit certificate or degree program. The training program was ready in September 1987. Current contracts exist with several companies, state and federal government agencies, and other organizations. The college developed its own introductory session, a project team training program, and workshops on various tools needed to implement TQM. Many of our administrators trained to implement Total Quality Management at DCCC teach in the external, contracted training program. DCCC staff who need training take the company training sessions. Between the internal applications and the external training, a good synergy is developing. The College Advisory System developed and approved a certificate program in Total Quality Management to begin in January 1991.

Part III: Implement TQM Throughout the Teaching and Learning Process. The targeted time period for this part of the plan is 1989–1996.

The employment of TQM techniques to improve teaching and learning is beginning at DCCC. A few teachers made the first informal applications by experimenting in their own classes. During the 1989–90 academic year, nursing faculty used TQM to study an alternative teaching approach in the simulation lab, with positive results. The learning outcomes were good, and the faculty liked using TQM techniques to solve a nagging problem. A group of faculty developed a grant proposal to adapt TQM to the teaching and learning process. Faculty involvement is voluntary, with increasing interest among some faculty. During this part of the implementation process, the college administration intends to be patient and involve faculty as they show interest.

The DCCC Experience

Problems and Pitfalls. It is not easy to adapt TQM to the college environment. Fundamental differences exist between education and business, and these differences make the prevailing model difficult to implement. However, the DCCC staff learned in its early TQM training that colleges and businesses have more similarities than differences. The greatest difficulty may lie in adapting TQM to the teaching and learning process, a phase DCCC is just beginning to enter.

The press of daily work inhibited implementation at first. The college staff is lean, and in the beginning, using the TQM methodology consumed considerable time because learning and doing occurred simultaneously. As a result, staff were reluctant to become involved. Convincing staff to use TQM requires time, constancy of purpose, and consistency of effort.

Some of the initial projects were too complex for a short-term project team. The I-team learned how to select and define projects to achieve improvements in a reasonable amount of time. For instance, projects came to focus on a single process controlled by one department. Finally, the I-team underestimated the resistance of people to fundamental change. Early progress could have been greater if the agents of this change had known what to expect.

Although some expressed values held in higher education are compatible with the TQM philosophy, few colleges have practiced those values in day-to-day operations. DCCC suffered some initial setbacks because, as resistant critics watched, some actions occurred that were at odds with TQM values and practices. For example, some unilateral personnel actions were taken that were at odds with the participatory values of TQM. As a result, skeptics could not resist pointing out the shortcomings of an administration that was struggling to transform itself. None of this helped the cause, and the administration learned to be more consistent in its adherence to TQM. Constancy of purpose is helping to overcome some of the resistance.

Products and Benefits. After four and a half years of experience, what has happened at DCCC in implementing TQM? There is heightened interest in the continuous improvement of processes. Although DCCC staff may not yet view problems as the "mountains of treasures" that some Japanese managers reportedly call them, staff in many departments are identifying problems with more enthusiasm than in prior years.

Staff members are paying more attention to defining a problem or objective carefully, identifying possible causal factors, collecting data, using proper analytical tools, verifying the important causes, and pilot testing actions before attempting full implementation. As noted earlier, the college is even following this model in its self-study for reaccreditation.

One of the axioms of TQM is that no improvement can occur unless there are known standards and measures to guide what you do and gauge where you are. In other words, without stable, standardized systems and processes yielding predictable results, there is no way of knowing with certainty if the intended results or improvements are being achieved. One of the important benefits of implementing TQM is that college staff are actively involving one another in a process of documenting and standardizing college operating procedures. In many cases procedures had wandered far from their intended purposes.

Colleges are notoriously poor in providing staff development. More staff development is occurring at DCCC since this transformation began. Staff are more willing to work in teams and across departments. The college is slowly removing barriers to teamwork. Staff members are seeing each other as "customers" or "suppliers" more readily. There is a growing recognition that the improvements we seek include both large and small ones. At the administrative level, initiatives include more careful planning using the TQM planning tools.

The executive staff at DCCC is convinced that TQM is worth every effort we have made. The college is on the leading edge of a management revolution designed to provide higher quality to keep the United States competitive. Success in implementing TQM will allow DCCC to continue to meet the needs of its stakeholders well into the next century.

Impact of TQM on the Institutional Research Office

During the first two years of implementation, the institutional research (IR) office activity centered on learning the philosophy, concepts, and tools of TQM and assisting with college staff training. Now the IR office is more involved in supporting the external training provided for local business, industry, service, and government organizations, since the need for direct teaching of college staff has diminished.

The involvement of college staff in trying to apply TQM increased the demand on the IR office for support in all phases of data collection, analysis, and interpretation. The function of the IR office changes as more college staff see themselves as internal customers identifying their own needs for research assistance. Rather than serving primarily as a source of reports, the IR office has evolved toward a consultative function and increasingly serves as a source of direction and assistance to staff engaged in their own research. Although the IR office helps college staff to define requests for information in operational terms, the ultimate responsibility lies with the staff person (or team) making the request. The result is more efficient and effective use of the resources available in the IR office. Because the internal customers of the IR office are actively involved in the "plan" phase of the plan-do-check-act process, they are better able to identify the data they need. A secondary benefit is that ownership of the data transfers to the person or team closest to the process being studied.

Another major change is the attempt to apply TQM to the daily operation of the IR office. For example, flowcharts identify and display steps in regularly scheduled projects. A data collection system documents key features of each request coming into the office. The patterns detected by analyzing these data are useful in planning future timetables and in identifying the office's internal customers and their information needs. Key TQM concepts (such as the distinction between normal random variation in processes and unusual nonrandom variation in processes) were introduced to virtually all administrators in the internal training. As a result, the office can use this common language to help administrators distinguish between the predictable variation of a stable process and the unpredictable variation that characterizes an unstable process. This distinction is crucial in determining when management action to improve a process is appropriate (Deming, 1986).

The application of individual tools is less important than the evolution toward a *Kaizen* attitude—that is, a commitment to constant improvement of quality (Imai, 1986)—about regular activities, projects, and processes. IR office staff try to approach each process with an eye to using previous experience in order to identify opportunities for improvement. This new attitude enables staff to take their implicit knowledge of routine systems and procedures and make it explicit by documenting steps and procedures. Documentation makes the process visible and brings to the surface targets for improvement: redundancy, complexity, rework, or bottlenecks. For example, a flowchart of an annual, countywide high school senior survey revealed how the process bogged down in the final stage, eventually requiring extra resources to get the job done. The following year a new method removed several steps in the process that did not contribute to its "real work" (Fuller, 1985). As a result, the project was completed three months earlier, without the extra staff time required during the previous year. In fact, the office was able to send to each high school an additional report to help the schools with required reporting to the state Department of Education.

It was undeniably difficult to identify IR office applications of TQM at first. However, with the transformation in managerial thinking, the applications became evident and appear to be limitless. The long-range benefits include more effective and efficient use of office resources, increased collaborative activity with administrators and faculty on issues of long-standing concern to the college, and a better understanding of the constantly changing information needs of the college community.

Conclusion

Verbal commitment to Total Quality Management is easier than implementation. Top personnel must show constancy of purpose to convince others that TQM can and will happen and that it is not just the latest management fad. Implementation requires patience, because it seems to take an interminable length of time for anything significant to happen. Without patience, the resulting frustration would undermine the transformation process. TQM represents a revolution in management philosophy but an evolution in implementation. With constancy of purpose and great patience, the transformation eventually begins to happen, sometimes in pleasantly surprising ways.

References

Deming, W. E. *Out of the Crisis*. Cambridge: Massachusetts Institute of Technology, Center for Advanced Engineering Study, 1986.

Fuller, F. T. "Eliminating Complexity from Work: Improving Productivity by Enhancing Quality." *National Productivity Review*, 1985, *4*, 327–344.

Imai, M. *Kaizen: The Key to Japan's Competitive Success*. New York: Random House, 1986.

Walton, M. *The Deming Management Method*. New York: Putnam, 1986.

Richard D. DeCosmo is president of Delaware County Community College.

Jerome S. Parker is dean of planning, research, and enrollment management at Delaware County Community College.

Mary Ann Heverly is director of institutional research at Delaware County Community College.

Oregon State began its adventure in Total Quality Management in 1989 and will never be the same!

Implementing Total Quality Management in a University Setting

L. Edwin Coate

This chapter tells the story of Oregon State University's (OSU) implementation of Total Quality Management (TQM), focusing on what OSU has learned in its quest for improved quality throughout its structure. OSU implemented Total Quality Management in nine phases. The discussion of each phase pays particular attention to lessons learned from mistakes, structural changes that evolved from the program, and changes in the behavior and attitudes of the participants.

Phase One: Exploring Total Quality Management

The purposes of phase one were to create a critical mass of top management people who would understand what TQM is and why it might be of use to the university and to determine who would be willing to test the concept in the university. We took this step because the vision of improved quality offered by TQM seemed to offer great potential and because the university was facing such major challenges as unhappy customers, a lack of resources, and low employee morale.

Activities Pursued. During phase one, activities included visits to excellent companies with TQM programs, including Ford, Hewlett-Packard, and Dow, whose chief executive officers are alumni of OSU. We invited W. Edwards Deming to visit the university to explain TQM and awarded him an honorary doctorate in June 1989. The university president and three other top managers attended an OSU continuing education class on the seven TQM tools taught by Hewlett-Packard TQM staff. Finally, we reviewed the criteria for the Malcolm Baldrige National Quality Award, which companies often use to implement and evaluate TQM programs (National Institute of Standards and Technology, 1991).

What We Learned. At the conclusion of phase one, the president and cabinet were enthusiastic about the potential of TQM. However, as word of these activities began to circulate, skepticism surfaced on the academic side of the university. Faculty saw TQM as the latest fad in management style. They strenuously objected to such TQM terminology as *total quality* and *management* and felt that if TQM were implemented, they might lose control of important academic processes.

At this point, some people attempted to change the TQM title to something more palatable—and proposed the name "System Improvement Process." But this simply generated suspicion and reinforced the idea that, by any name, the new approach was another management fad.

Generally, faculty members see themselves as emphasizing diversity. To them, the idea of quality control suggests uniformity—an attempt to bring everything to the same level. In addition, many faculty members are accustomed to working alone, to competing, in fact, for limited resources such as grant money. Gaining acceptance on the academic side for the idea of working in teams may be a challenge at any university.

Gradually, however, some members of the academic community began to give qualified approval to TQM. One said that "the great value I see in this concept is it will change our orientation to seeing students as customers. This will require a turnaround in our culture." In fact, TQM teams are now working in two academic service-oriented areas: international education and continuing education.

For many reasons, we decided to proceed slowly on the academic side. We targeted service units as the place to begin, since these units have many parallels with industry in such areas as physical plant, computing, and business services. The next step was to initiate a pilot project in the physical plant department.

Phase Two: Establishing a Pilot Study Team

In order to apply what we knew about TQM and to learn more, OSU formed a TQM study team in the physical plant. The team's charge was to address a specific, high-priority issue that had a high probability of success, that management agreed was important, that was a project on which no one was working, and that was important to the customer.

At the time the TQM study team was formed, OSU's physical plant department had poor internal communication and low worker morale. The department's image among many of its customers was extremely negative: Services were slow, expensive, and delivered with little concern for customers' needs or desires.

The TQM Process. The pilot study team included managers and front-line workers, a team leader, and a training officer who was a facilitator, for a total of twelve. The issue the team studied was how to "decrease turn-around time in the remodeling process." Moving through the TQM process, the team opened communication within the entire department, briefed other employees on progress, published team minutes, and posted its "process flow diagram" on the office wall for comments and suggestions.

Team members found overlaps, time delays, and unnecessary paper flow in the remodeling process. They came to realize that their issue, though solvable, required studying too many facets. (The process flow diagram, if laid out in a straight line, would have been seventeen feet long.) The team also found that a key area, engineering, needed more representation. To solve these problems, the team leader formed two subteams in engineering design and construction. These groups identified problems in their processes, brainstormed causes, and proposed solutions to the pilot study team.

Results. Solutions implemented through TQM changed the basic structure of the physical plant staff and shortened the remodeling process initially by 10 percent and, after a second phase of study, by 23 percent. Changes included establishing a customer service center and creating the position of project manager, both of which improved responsiveness to customer inquiries. Other time-saving tactics are now being implemented.

New Attitudes. The establishment of TQM teams in the physical plant has resulted in tremendous changes in work relationships and attitudes. The process showed top managers internal problems that they had not recognized before and exposed workers to problems that managers face in day-to-day operations. The result is cooperation.

Because team members came from all levels of the organization, they were able to improve internal communication. Shortly after the first team was formed, word filtered out to the shops that things were changing for the better. Shops began talking with each other, and coordinating projects became much easier.

Physical plant has become a much better place to work, employees say. Networks are spreading across the entire work force, and workers are making many suggestions for improvements. With worker cooperation, areas that have had too many or too few employees are being reorganized.

One factor that is not measurable, according to the TQM team leader, is a change in the work ethic. People are conscious of possibilities for improvement. They are doing a better job. The overall results have been happier customers and more trusting relationships among workers.

A survey of customers showed that, even in projects where the time to completion has not decreased, they are more satisfied and more understanding of delays. Customers see that the physical plant department is concerned and working on its problems. Customers feel that they are important because the physical plant department listens to them and they are getting more personalized services.

Phase Three: Defining Customer Needs

Quality function deployment (QFD) is an organized system that identifies and ranks customer needs and translates them into university priorities (GOAL/QPC Research Committee, 1990b). QFD is also a strategic tool in which customer needs and the characteristics of a service system are pulled into a matrix to see whether they match.

OSU began QFD by identifying customers and placing them into major groupings. The external customers include students who attend OSU, students who do not attend OSU, community, legislature, parents, visitors, system chancellor, alumni, international community, grantors, other institutions, and the state board of higher education. Internal customers include supervisors, faculty, staff, and co-workers.

Tools such as customer surveys, focus groups, complaints, comments, and others helped OSU to identify customer needs. Through data analysis we formed a comprehensive set of customer views. This information helped executive management to understand customers' perceptions and expectations of the university. It also highlighted points where data on customer needs and expectations are incomplete or nonexistent.

Three surveys conducted in 1989-90 provided data about OSU's customers. The OSU Image Survey evaluated the perceived images of Oregon State University in the minds of six important customer groups: the general public, college-bound Oregon high school students, OSU alumni living in Oregon, OSU undergraduate students, classified staff, and faculty. The following are some of the survey's findings:

1. About one-third of the general public, one-sixth of prospective students, and nearly one-half of the alumni are not knowledgeable about OSU, its programs, and activities.

2. The physical attractiveness of OSU received the highest ratings; and while most groups perceived a friendly atmosphere, students, alumni, staff, and faculty gave low ratings to the concern of the OSU administration in dealing with their needs.

3. Customers in the general public gave OSU good ratings in providing such services to the state as preparing graduates to be useful employees, listening to Oregonians, and helping citizens solve their problems.

4. In general, customers rated OSU's academic reputation as average, with recruitment of top students and matters of rigor and requirements rated low.

The Admitted Students Survey gave additional information about student customers, both those who did and did not enroll at OSU. Respondents compared OSU with other institutions they considered. In the area of information provided about OSU, they gave lowest marks to financial aid communications, college-sponsored meetings, contact with faculty, and contact with coaches. Contact with students and campus visits were rated highest. The images of OSU most frequently cited were friendly, social, comfortable, and fun.

The 1990 Faculty Survey provided the following information about the university's internal academic customers: Their highest professional goal is to be good teachers, and their undergraduate teaching goal is to develop students' ability to think clearly; their highest-priority issues for the university are promoting intellectual development and conducting basic applied research; job satisfaction centers mainly on having autonomy and independence, and time pressures are the greatest source of stress; the primary funding priority is salaries, with support services, including facilities repair and library, ranking second.

Results. The results of these studies revealed that OSU needs to reassess its reluctance to engage in marketing. The idea of designing classes and courses to fit the market has been foreign to the university's way of thinking. A change in attitudes is necessary in order to succeed in the marketplace. OSU has created a marketing committee to look at its image and the products it delivers—a first step in beginning to realign classes to meet client needs.

The marketing committee will become one of the first cross-functional teams. Training will help the team understand TQM concepts and carry out quality function deployment activities. Because of the lack of nonindustry examples (most QFD examples focus on automobile designs), OSU may have problems in utilizing this concept. Total commitment to developing customer-driven systems will not come easily.

Phase Four: Adopting the Breakthrough Planning Process

The breakthrough (Hoshin) planning process has five major steps (GOAL/ QPC Research Committee, 1990a).

Step 1: Define Mission. All universities have a teaching mission; because OSU is a land-grant and sea-grant university, it also has a mission to conduct research and provide service. Hence the mission statement reads: "OSU's mission as a land-grant university is to serve the people of Oregon, the nation, and the world through education, research, and service."

Step 2: Understand Customers. Customers are becoming increasingly conscious of value. To become a leader in the future educational marketplace, OSU needs to establish itself firmly as the supplier of the highest value, the one most responsive to its customers' expectations. This means evaluating everything OSU does in terms of the value provided to the university's external customers. It means asking customers about their expec-

Table 1. OSU's Twelve Critical Processes

Process	Performance Measure
1. Admissions	Concordance with enrollment management plan
2. Curriculum development	Peer acceptance
3. Teaching	Student teaching evaluation
4. International development	Number of students going overseas
5. Research	Number of publications
6. Service delivery (extension)	Percent of community participation
7. Community relations	Number of complaints
8. Information services	Computer-student ratio
9. Long-range planning	Percent of objectives met
10. Work force hiring and development	Percent of first-choice hires
11. Facilities development	Percent of value to money for repairs
12. Funding development	Money obtained versus money requested

tations and taking action to meet those expectations. It also means continually monitoring customer satisfaction.

Step 3: Identify Critical Processes. Identifying the president's critical processes—the functions essential to accomplishing the university's mission—lays the foundation for the TQM process. To do this, OSU identified the president's principal customers and the services the university provides to each customer group, and then identified the key critical processes for these groups. The twelve processes and their performance measures are shown in Table 1. OSU also integrated its detailed statement of goals and objectives with its critical processes.

Step 4: State the Vision. OSU's vision began to take shape with the creation of an affinity diagram (Brassard, 1989) that collected attributes of the ideal university and organized them into sets of related information. Discussions about why senior managers may hold different views about the desired characteristics of their university in the future helped to highlight the uniqueness of OSU and its mission. The university's statement of its mission, values, and guiding principles formed the basis for its vision statement:

> It is OSU's vision to be recognized as a premier international university. We want each student to have at least one additional language, to have at least one quarter's experience in a foreign country, and to be computer literate. We want our faculty to have international experience and to increase our international research programs by 100 percent (from twenty-six countries now to fifty-two). We want to increase foreign undergraduates from 10 to 15 percent of the student body.
>
> We also want our university to be the best university in which to study and work. We want to be a university that knows what its clients

will want ten years from now and what it will do to exceed all expectations. We want to be a university whose employees understand not only how to do their jobs but also how to significantly improve their jobs on a regular basis; where problems and challenges are met by a team of the most appropriate people, regardless of their level or jobs in the university.

After completing the vision statement, attention shifted to identifying barriers to achieving it. Using the affinity diagram process again, OSU explored characteristics of the barriers, then used another TQM tool, the spider diagram (Collett, 1990), to prioritize them. The purpose of this analysis is to develop actions to remove the barriers that might keep OSU from attaining its vision. Our barriers included a deteriorating physical infrastructure, the increasing costs of doing research, a deteriorating public image, deteriorating staff morale, and inadequate information systems (computing, library, and telecommunications).

Step 5: Identify Priority Breakthrough Items. Breakthrough items are activities geared to generate quality improvements in systems and procedures. Using the vision statement, the statement of goals and objectives, and the barriers identified in step four, OSU focused on key breakthrough areas of service. TQM's breakthrough planning does not replace the university's strategic plan but supplements it by ensuring that employees at all levels understand their role in achieving the vision, deploying the plan to the department level and ensuring that each academic or support department develops targets and strategies for reaching the vision, providing detailed plans for support and measurement of progress toward the vision, and providing more operations detail than most traditional plans offer.

A five-step process identified three priority breakthrough items: increase computing capability in the university, increase internationalization of the university, and increase administrative efficiency by implementing TQM. OSU then developed a preliminary five-year plan based on the assessment and selection of priority breakthrough items and the Baldrige Award criteria.

What We Learned. Breakthrough planning is a logical extension of strategic planning, and the planning process went smoothly. The president's participation in extensive planning sessions and in the successive modification of plans was essential. The president was surprised to discover that the implementation of TQM in all facets of university life would take five years. This discovery required the president to make a significant, long-term commitment to the TQM process.

Phase Five: Performing Breakthrough Planning in the Divisions

Following the process employed by the president's cabinet, the vice-president and the division directors of finance and administration created a vision statement, revised their mission statements, and identified nine critical processes for their divisions. The goals and objectives previously developed as part of OSU's management-by-objectives process were then distributed among the division directors. The major breakthrough item was to implement TQM throughout finance and administration.

Phase Six: Forming Daily Management Teams

Teams are at the heart of TQM. Better solutions emerge when everyone involved has a chance to work on process problems. Equally important, solutions are implemented faster and last longer because the people affected have helped to develop them.

Each study team should be composed of no more than ten people who normally work together on the process being reviewed and who control the resources necessary to improve that process. Each team has a sponsor, usually the group's division director, who ensures that the team's work is linked to the critical processes and moves the institution toward its vision.

Team Roles. If teamwork is to be successful, team members must clearly understand their roles from the outset. The team leader, typically the supervisor, is responsible for planning meetings, establishing constraints, distributing agendas in advance, keeping minutes, communicating with the sponsor, and ensuring that the team completes its action plans. The facilitator makes problem-solving suggestions, helps the team stay focused, provides "just-in-time" training on the problem-solving process, and ensures that everyone has a chance to participate. The team member attends all meetings, contributes ideas, collects data, recommends solutions, and helps to implement them.

Problem-Solving Process. Teams make improvements by following a ten-step problem-solving process designed to provide a common technique and language for process improvement. The process begins with the customer, focuses on root causes and barriers to improvement, and ensures that decisions and actions are based on real data.

Step One. The sponsor identifies and selects the most important opportunities for improvement. OSU started with critical processes, especially those that support its goals, objectives, and breakthrough items. The sponsor selects team members and empowers them to make improvements. The team carries out the remaining steps.

Step Two. The team determines the key customers of the targeted processes and the services provided them. Then it surveys the customers, using a standard format, and analyzes the survey data using specific TQM tools such as check sheets and Pareto diagrams.

Step Three. The team selects the most important issue, the area that customers say most needs improvement, and writes a clear issue statement.

Step Four. The team identifies and flowcharts the key process or processes. This enables the team to recognize opportunities for improvement.

Step Five. The team decides which aspects of performance to measure and sets goals for continuous improvement in meeting or exceeding customer expectations. To achieve this, the team must evaluate current performance realistically and set attainable goals for improvement.

Step Six. The team begins to explore probable causes of the problems and barriers to improvement. A cause-and-effect diagram may be useful here.

Step Seven. The team gathers data on the probable causes of problems. The information gives the team a benchmark against which to measure its future progress.

Step Eight. The team evaluates the data and shows it pictorially in charts and graphs.

Step Nine. The team brainstorms and develops permanent solutions. It implements solutions, monitors their performance, and adopts them if they work.

Step Ten. If the problem is solved, the team standardizes the solutions as normal operating procedures.

OSU formed teams in each division of finance and administration around one of that division's critical processes—if possible, a process that dealt with a university objective. For example, the printing division team took information services as its critical process and produced the following issue statement: "to reduce the amount of time in the prepress stage of the printing process." As a second example, the human resources division chose work-force hiring and development and produced this statement: "to increase the speed of initial response in the information dissemination process."

International education, continuing education, housing, and development are also forming study teams. The academic area formed a steering committee to begin implementing TQM. Ultimately, all OSU employees will be on a TQM team; this will require about 400 teams.

What We Learned. The finance and administration TQM study teams offer the following comments on the problem-solving process based on their experiences.

Surveys and Flowcharts. The parts of the problem-solving process that members found most valuable were the customer survey and the flowchart. Surveys helped team members get to know their customers as people. The flowchart often helped them visualize the process for the first time. Teams used a standard computer software package called "Easy Flow" (© Haven Tree Software Limited) to create their diagrams.

Issues. All ten teams changed their issue statements from the original formulations provided by the teams' sponsors. Many teams commented that they would prefer to choose their own issue rather than have one assigned.

Team Diversity. Each team used the tools of the TQM process in the way that best fit its situation. Some moved rapidly, others more cautiously. Some teams felt pressured and hurried by their sponsors, leaders, and facilitators. Other teams felt they were moving too slowly and wanted to rush ahead. Evidently, sponsors and other managers need to accept that each team will operate in its own fashion at its own speed.

Time. Many team members remarked that the team meetings and study assignments left them too little time to perform their regular duties. Sponsors must show their commitment to TQM by helping team members adjust their schedules accordingly.

Training. Many facilitators and team leaders and some team members felt inadequately trained to accomplish their roles effectively.

Despite these criticisms, team members reacted favorably overall. They appreciated that teams were formed at all levels of the organization, and they felt that they had seen improvements in both their own and other departments.

Phase Seven: Initiating Cross-Functional Pilot Projects

Frequently, difficult problems and opportunities lie across several functional areas. The purpose of cross-functional teams is to target team efforts on key projects that cross functional lines, to integrate studies that cover several divisions, and to evaluate and improve the work of ongoing study teams. Cross-functional teams can also select projects aligned with the priority breakthrough items.

OSU's pilot cross-functional team, composed of division directors of finance and administration, selected the issue of improving the study team process. The team surveyed its customers (the other study team members, sponsors, and facilitators), identified causes of problems in two areas— developing issue statements and training—and is beginning to test solutions.

Phase Eight: Implementing Cross-Functional Total Quality Management

The cross-functional pilot project is still under way but promises excellent results and applications. Universities operate with many committees that are composed of faculty, staff, and students. Most such committees have cross-functional responsibilities and, with the necessary training, are ideal vehicles for implementing TQM at a cross-functional level.

Phase Nine: Setting Up Reporting, Recognition, and Awards Systems

Each division director reports monthly to the vice-president for finance and administration. The reports focus on the performance measures of each division director's critical processes. During yearly reviews of critical process improvements, the vice president sets the next year's goals for the director. These performance evaluations are tied to salary evaluations with improvements reflected in salary increases.

As study teams finish their work on an issue, the vice-president and the division directors meet as a review committee and hear the team present its solutions and the team sponsor report on progress in implementing those solutions. Teams also report to the president and his cabinet as a demonstration of senior management interest in TQM. This also provides immediate recognition of team members. However, most team members find that the implementation of their solutions is the best reward possible; hence, the tracking of implementation is an important part of the OSU reporting and recognition program.

OSU is also developing an awards program to recognize outstanding performances by both teams and individuals. The criteria for selection include originality of solutions, amount of savings in terms of time and money, and importance to the university. Three categories of awards will be presented; each category is open to any employee, and any employee can make nominations.

Conclusion and Recommendations

In creating Oregon State's vision statement, the university identified Total Quality Management as vital not only for the realization of its vision but also for its continued survival in the marketplace. Quality is what customers say it is, not what universities tell them it is. Both internal and external customers want to receive the same high-quality service at all times, with no surprises. Progress can only be determined and improved by measurement.

Although TQM is a relatively simple concept, putting it to work in a university setting has proved challenging. The language of TQM comes from the manufacturing industry, not education, and the teamwork approach to problem solving is unfamiliar to most midlevel managers. Nonetheless, TQM is considered a success at OSU, where twenty teams are operating with significant results. It has saved the university time, reduced costs, empowered people at all levels, and improved morale.

Based on OSU's experience, the successful implementation of TQM in a college or university setting depends on observing the six key principles listed in these concluding paragraphs.

Support from the Top. It is essential to have a firm commitment to TQM from the president or chief operating officer of the university. Deming (1986) found this to be the single most important step in implementing TQM throughout an organization.

Find a Champion. Implementing TQM requires a long-term commitment (five years), a lot of time (up to 20 percent of the normal workload), and money (at least $60,000 per year). A person with considerable authority must champion TQM from inception to implementation.

Act. Do not research TQM too exhaustively. Learn about the steps necessary to form and operate a team, then start one. Only by practical experience can an institution discover how TQM really operates.

Teams Are Everything. The essence of TQM is the study team devoted to process improvement. Make sure that teams are adequately trained. The TQM process will ensure that solutions are implemented.

Breakthrough Planning Helps. Although not included in all TQM programs, breakthrough planning helps align departments, integrate the existing strategic planning processes, and focus effort on processes that can make a difference.

Try the Service Side First. In a university, the service side is an easier place to start implementing TQM than is the academic side. Begin with a unit that is having trouble, that recognizes it needs help, and that will appreciate being helped. Early success is necessary to develop momentum.

References

Brassard, M. *The Memory Jogger Plus+*. Methuen, Mass.: GOAL/QPC, 1989.

Collett, C. 1990. (For information on the spider chart, contact Catherine Collett, Collett and Associates, 5176 Metge Avenue, Albany, Oregon 97321.)

Deming, W. E. *Out of the Crisis*. Cambridge: Massachusetts Institute of Technology, Center for Advanced Engineering Study, 1986.

GOAL/QPC Research Committee. *Hoshin Planning: A Planning System for Implementing Total Quality Management (TQM)*. Methuen, Mass.: GOAL/QPC, 1990a.

GOAL/QPC Research Committee. *Quality Function Deployment: A Process for Translating Customers' Needs into a Better Product and Profit*. Methuen, Mass.: GOAL/QPC, 1990b.

National Institute of Standards and Technology. 1991 Application Guidelines, Malcolm Baldrige National Quality Award. Gaithersburg, Md.: National Institute of Standards and Technology, 1991.

L. Edwin Coate is vice-president for finance and administration at Oregon State University.

TQM and assessment have much in common; a lot can be learned from comparing their philosophies, methods, and experiences.

Assessment and TQM:
In Search of Convergence

Peter T. Ewell

Both supporters and critics have drawn parallels between Total Quality Management (TQM) and the current assessment movement in higher education. Assessment practitioners, while intrigued by TQM, are frequently put off by its obvious linguistic and methodological links to industrial production processes that appear to have little to do with teaching and learning. New converts to TQM within the academy, in turn, have been critical of assessment because it appears to rely exclusively on "inspection at the end point" as a lever for quality improvement. Because proponents on both sides are enthusiastic about their own approaches, they sometimes do not listen to one another carefully, nor do they often watch what the practitioners of the other approach actually do. The result, I believe, obscures important lessons both sides might learn from a linking of these two powerful and basically allied approaches.

My purpose in this chapter is to address this condition in three ways. First, I want to demonstrate some clear conceptual parallels between the two approaches. TQM and assessment have similar objectives and origins. What divides them, I believe, is a peculiar set of historical circumstances surrounding public accountability in higher education. Second, I want to show how evolving assessment practice at the institutional and unit level is consistent with the best tenets of TQM. Assessment has taught us hard lessons about the need to collect information on both processes and outcomes. The need to link assessment information directly with the academic workplace—that is, with individual units and classrooms—is an equally hard lesson. Moreover, emerging assessment practice also now emphasizes "hearing the student's voice"—a welcome, though somewhat belated, embodiment of customer consciousness. All three trends make the emerging practice of assessment far different at present from its popular early image of end-point standardized testing. Finally, both assessment and TQM, as mechanisms for academic improvement, face some substantial common obstacles. If either is to prosper, each must systematically recognize and address these obstacles.

Assessment as a "Quality Movement"

The emergence of assessment as a national phenomenon in higher education is generally marked by the publication of two national reports: *Involvement in Learning* (National Institute of Education, 1984) and *Integrity in the College Curriculum* (Association of American Colleges, 1985). Both called for reform, including major changes in curricular coverage and coherence. In this sense the two differ little in content from similar bouts of reconceptualization that have afflicted American undergraduate education. But both reports also called for a fresh look at the undergraduate product—particularly at the array of knowledge, skills, and attitudes that all recipients of the baccalaureate should possess in common. Embedded in this admonition was something new: that regular feedback about performance was a key to improvement. At the individual level, considerable research about the dynamics of active learning backed this proposition (Astin, 1977, 1985). At the institutional level, the implied argument about assessment was more radical: Information about results, if gathered frequently at all levels of the organization, might guide a continuous process of organizational learning. The resulting "self-regarding institution" (Ewell, 1984) is infused with information about performance at all levels, thus constantly monitoring and improving its own overall performance.

But assessment, like TQM, also arose in part from a perception of crisis. Members of the National Institute of Education's (NIE's) study group, for example, were well aware that they were following in the footsteps of significant and far more critical reviews of elementary and secondary education, such as that issued by the U.S. Department of Education (1983). At the same time, higher education could no longer ignore complaints from business and industry about the declining quality of baccalaureate graduates. By 1986, the momentum of external reform had reached higher education. Reports by the Education Commission of the States (ECS) (1986) and the National Governors' Association (NGA) (1986) signaled government's growing unwillingness to remain on the sidelines with respect to undergraduate quality.

Government also saw assessment as a major component of reform. The ECS and NGA reports argued for gathering evidence at the institutional level to guide continuous improvement. But they also called for institutions to report statistics that would tell potential student "customers" what they might expect to gain from colleges and universities and that would assure the public that higher education was managing public investment well. As a result, the reports encouraged states to develop and deploy assessment initiatives that could both stimulate local reform and provide increased accountability. Because of the latter requirement, however, such systems tended by nature to emphasize assessment by inspection. In many cases, reports proposed standardized testing and included institutional comparisons as a part of the assessment program design.

Today's assessment movement is complicated largely because of these two different origins, one within higher education and the other external. Both advocated the same set of techniques—as a "market reaction" by state government to declining customer satisfaction and as an internal improvement tool by colleges and universities to help make a better product. For the most part, the typical current pattern of state initiatives avoids the implied contradictions of these two agendas. Rather than calling for uniform outcomes testing, as was largely the case in kindergarten through twelfth-grade education, the majority of current higher education assessment mandates are decentralized and enabling (Ewell, Finney, and Lenth, 1990). State authorities require institutions to develop local assessment programs suited to their own diverse missions and student clienteles and to report results periodically. Within broadly established guidelines, authorities allow many assessment methodologies provided that they generate understandable evidence of effectiveness for their respective constituencies. State authorities are often aware, to a surprising extent, of the need to avoid "micro-management" in developing such policies (Ewell, 1990). In this sense, they strongly subscribe to current quality management theory. But current evidence suggests that their patience is also limited; if institutions do not take the initiative in developing appropriate local reforms, state authorities feel that they have no choice but to deploy stronger, more centralized assessment methods to address the "crisis."

The state, for better or worse, remains the primary buyer of public higher education's product. As such, it in many ways plays the role the market plays in private industry by providing the overriding stimulus for unit adaptation and reform. State-mandated assessment represents both a market signal to colleges and universities from its primary (though often its most unrecognized) customer and a critical tool for local improvement. Given these dual motives, it is no wonder that college and university officials are often confused about how to approach the task of assessment. But whatever the state's agenda, local assessment may prove valuable to institutions. In the best case, represented currently by such states as Virginia and Washington, state authorities will welcome and support local efforts at self-improvement. In the worst case, state-mandated testing for quality control (currently exemplified by Florida's College Level Academic Skills Test), local assessment may still be useful as a tool for quality improvement to meet externally established standards for product quality.

Convergence in Practice: Some Parallels

Emerging "best practice" in assessment, I believe, has much in common with the admonitions of TQM. Best practice, of course, has not as yet become common practice. Because most institutions currently engaging in assessment are doing so primarily to comply with state mandates, approaches that emphasize end-point inspection and purely quantitative criteria tend to predominate. More subtly, under these conditions assessment becomes the concern of administrators rather than faculty—particularly, as in states such as Virginia or Tennessee, where dollars are at stake.

Regardless of its external stimulus, moreover, a natural evolution of institutional assessment practice often occurs. Many first explore standardized testing alternatives because they are both readily available and apparently credible; few faculty are initially willing to invest the level of effort required to develop the kinds of course-embedded methods essential for guiding continuous instructional improvement. Only after experiencing the limitations of test-based assessment is the institution often willing to try alternative approaches. At institutions such as King's College (Wilkes-Barre, Pennsylvania), Northeast Missouri State University, State University of New York at Plattsburg, or the University of Tennessee at Knoxville—all of which have been practicing assessment for five years or more—initially established end-point testing is now complemented by a growing range of input and behavioral measures.

Three trends in particular now characterize emerging best practice in assessment, and all, I believe, are consistent with the tenets of TQM. First, comprehensive assessment programs rely increasingly on systematic process indicators to make sense of observed outcomes. Second, assessment relies increasingly on naturalistic settings as the locus for information gathering. Finally, a trend is growing in assessment toward simple techniques that enable line faculty to gather and use information directly about how their classrooms are actually functioning.

Rediscovering Process. Early attempts to assess instructional outcomes in higher education rested strongly on the assumption that instructional processes were uniform. The critical job was to document results in a systematic and comparable way—a substantially neglected task up to that point. The primary methodological paradigm for assessment in this period was the psychological experiment: causally linking planned and systematic variations in treatment conditions to observed differences in outcomes. Trying to make sense of obtained results, however, quickly made it clear that enormous and unknown variations in "treatment" were probably most responsible for differences in outcomes. We cannot treat instructional processes in colleges and universities simply as assigned conditions in a stable experimental design.

To some extent, this obvious "discovery" was an artifact of procedure. In developing assessments, conventional wisdom held it necessary to begin with a clear statement of intended outcomes. Without a common set of instructional goals, assessment was impossible in principle. Most college faculty had never engaged in goal making of this kind; often, in fact, they found reaching such an agreement more controversial even than measuring outcomes. For many, the resulting discussions themselves provided new insights into optimal program design (Banta and Moffett, 1987). After faculty had agreed on goals, however, it quickly became legitimate to ask who was teaching which of them, where, how, and at the same time raise behavioral questions about the ways in which the curricula on paper actually were acted out.

Current assessment practice, in response to these concerns, is devoting particular attention to collecting information about instructional process. One approach documents patterns of student course taking. Because the majority of current college curricula are choice-based and because most computerized student records systems are exclusively term-oriented, institutions often have remarkably little knowledge of their "behavioral curricula"—the actual sequence of courses taken to fulfill requirements. In the absence of such knowledge, of course, meaningful interpretation of outcomes is problematic. The construction of "curricular maps" as a part of this process is roughly equivalent to the common and essential TQM exercise of flowcharting (Ewell and Lisensky, 1988). Investigating the behavioral curriculum corresponds to TQM's necessary next step of documenting the actual flow of work. Basic tools here are transcript analysis and longitudinal student record files. In the first case, analysis is retrospective and often reveals substantial deviation in practice from intended catalogue design (Zemsky, 1989; Ratcliffe and Associates, 1990). Longitudinal tracking systems represent a more active alternative oriented toward continuous behavioral monitoring. To date, they have enjoyed their greatest success in community college settings, particularly in the improvement of placement and remediation practices (Adelman, Ewell, and Grable, 1989). In common with industrial experience, institutions in the latter case have often discovered that nothing is wrong with their current placement and remediation policies but that deficiencies occur because no one is actually following these policies.

Another process focus involves documenting student and instructor behavior. Research on student retention (and increasingly on student learning and development as well) has convincingly established that behavioral factors such as student involvement (Astin, 1985), quality of effort (Pace, 1984), and substantive direct interaction with faculty members outside a classroom setting (Terenzini and Pascarella, 1977) can be at least as important as curricular design in explaining successful outcomes. As a result, many institutions are experimenting with techniques that gather information directly from students about their use of time and about their in- and out-of-class behaviors and from faculty members about their teaching practices (Gamson and Poulsen, 1989). A widely used vehicle for gathering such information is the traditional end-of-course questionnaire generally used for faculty evaluation. Increasingly, institutions are adding items to these questionnaires that tap such factors as time on task (for example, the student's amount of out-of-class preparation per week), active learning (for example, the number of times the student actively raised questions in class, the number of times the student discussed class material with the instructor or peers, or whether the student sought out additional material on the topic from the library or other sources), or high standards (for example, whether or not students felt challenged by the course or felt they did their best). Other recent approaches center on directly investigating effective student and classroom behaviors. A recent example is the work of the Harvard Assessment Seminar that established the value of such practices as group study and frequent instructor feedback (Light, 1990).

A third trend is increased attention to establishing the concrete connections that occur across courses in a curriculum. Curricular engineering generally assumes a structure of implied or actual prerequisites for successful performance in a sequence of courses. But to what extent are learnings in a given course successfully applied in another, often after a lapse of several terms? Since we often teach basic skills, in general, without attempts to link them to the problem settings where they will most likely be used, answers to this question are particularly important. Before and after exercises to help assess the core course sequence at King's College are an example of how cross-course connections of this kind establish and improve course sequencing (Farmer, 1988). At the beginning of second-year core courses, for example, the exercises ask students to respond to questions explicitly designed to tap general skills taught at an earlier point in the sequence but cast in an alien setting. Where these transitions are not occurring, faculty are encouraged to work together to develop the appropriate skills in the needed context.

Do not read assessment's growing emphasis on process information of this kind as an abandonment of outcomes. Rather, the premise is to establish a reasonable set of baseline measures that can consistently monitor the overall quality of the instructional product. But we now recognize that outcome measures are only the beginning of a process that requires additional, highly disaggregated information about how and where learning takes place, as well as an active set of local intervention mechanisms for incremental improvement. Moreover, as the next section will explore, outcome measures themselves have changed. No longer are they strictly oriented toward endpoint testing; rather, they are now often embedded within the process, offering the opportunity for continuous improvement.

Using Naturalistic Inquiry in Assessment. Many early examples of assessment emphasized the use of standardized examinations. In the popular value-added rubric, for example, comparing end-point scores to entry scores assumes that any difference is due to instruction. In the more common examples of single-point testing, moreover, the objective is as much to certify the standard of the educational product as it is to improve practice. With both types of testing, assessment can be a costly external process that is imposed on the educational process and manifested in the form of specially designated test days and purpose-built instruments.

Recently, however, assessment practice has undergone a transformation similar to that experienced by program evaluation in the midseventies (Shapiro, 1986). Rather than relying on externally imposed measurement devices outside the classroom, assessment is becoming more naturalistic (Guba and Lincoln, 1981)—embedded directly within the processes that it seeks to understand. This recent evolution of practice is consistent with the tenets of TQM in two important ways. First, assessment is not for the most part a costly extra step imposed on the process from without and adding little value. Curriculum-embedded assessment, as practiced at Alverno College, for example (Mentkowski and Doherty, 1984), uses assessment techniques to make general inferences about process effectiveness and to correct detected deficiencies on the line before the process is over. Second, embedded assessment takes place at the level of practice. When assessment information is gathered through the creative use of existing classroom examinations and exercises, the results are seen in their appropriate context and are thus made immediately meaningful and applicable for faculty.

Three recent trends in naturalistic assessment are particularly noteworthy as parallels to TQM. The first involves identifying and exploiting a network of existing points of contact with students as appropriate vehicles for assessment. Rather than relying on specially constructed testing points to gather information, this approach emphasizes more effective utilization of existing but underutilized data-collection opportunities. Among these are registration and orientation, end-of-course teaching evaluation surveys, and existing student surveys—as well as a range of unobtrusive data-gathering devices. Consistent with TQM, often the first step is to flowchart the current process to identify all the points at which information about students is currently collected. The resulting map is not only valuable in planning the substance of assessment but the flowchart can also help to increase the efficiency of assessment substantially. Indeed, several colleges have found that this audit process results in net gains in informational efficiency—particularly with respect to student surveys—because the audit process typically uncovers so many duplicate and badly designed data-collection practices (Ewell and Lisensky, 1988).

A second practice, strongly resembling TQM's use of sampling, is to examine periodically examples of actual student work. The classic example is the portfolio that generally evaluates writing skills but that extends to other skill domains as well. To be successful, one must collect portfolios systematically, and the portfolios must contain similar kinds of student products: papers, essay test question responses, lab reports, or defined projects. Viewing the process as a regrading of large numbers of previously evaluated pieces of work subjects it to many of the same criticisms that TQM makes of other inspections. In fact, large numbers of institutions are currently experiencing enormous increases in assessment workload through the use of portfolios, precisely because they have not fully thought through the intended purposes. One of the most promising alternatives to mass portfolio collection is to choose work samples on a median performance basis. Under this methodology, administrators request instructors to forward for evaluation only the work of the median performer on each exercise; the result is a valuable periodic snapshot of assessed average performance across the curriculum.

A third naturalistic assessment practice consistent with TQM involves harnessing the faculty's own grading process to yield additional information more useful for instructional improvement. Course-embedded assessment, as practiced in general education at Kean College of New Jersey, for example, rests on the careful design of common essay items for periodic inclusion in course final examinations. Normally the faculty grades these items, but they also read a sample collectively, using an explicit scoring guide designed to detect overall patterns of strength and weakness. As a result of the scoring exercise, faculty course teams can determine how to address apparent weaknesses more systematically.

All three manifestations of naturalistic assessment have in common the assumption that the most useful information for improving practice is that which is most closely rooted in the processes it seeks to inform. Assessment has moved strongly in this direction not just because such practices are more acceptable to faculty members than are standardized tests but also because they are more applicable and informative. Carrying this logic to its extreme, however, implies that assessment will focus on individual classrooms, and this injunction has resulted in the assessment approaches, described next, that most strongly resemble TQM.

Using Assessment as Classroom Research. If naturalistic assessment calls attention to TQM's injunction that the best information is rooted in the operation of real, local processes, the emerging classroom research movement emphasizes TQM's equally important requirement that the workers themselves collect quality control information continuously. This enables individual instructors to help manage and direct their own instruction through an array of classroom feedback devices (Cross and Angelo, 1988). Advocates of classroom research believe that its potential to transform practice far exceeds that of more centralized, formal assessment procedures, both because individual faculty members manage it themselves and because it focuses largely on obtaining process information that faculty will find far less threatening than information about outcomes (Cross, 1990).

Like the control charts managed by individual production workers under TQM (Walton, 1986), the hallmark of classroom research techniques is their simplicity. While the techniques may require consistency in their application over time to be effective, faculty do not need a statistical or measurement background in order to use them. The most well-known example is the minute paper, intended to be administered to students at the end of every class period—a device that also recognizes the need for instructors to receive continuous customer feedback. The most common variant asks students to respond to two questions: What is the most important thing that you learned today, and what is the single thing that after today still is most unclear to you? The instructor collects the anonymous responses to the questions to help target instruction for the subsequent class period. Considerable experience with this technique (to this point primarily in community colleges) indicates that it can make a substantial contribution to instructor awareness about the effectiveness of presented material and, in contrast to the traditional end-of-course questionnaire, it makes this contribution in time to make a difference.

Most classroom research techniques are similar to the minute paper in their concentration on monitoring classroom process. Some, however, provide classroom counterparts for other familiar tools of statistical quality control. (For a description of these basic tools, see Appendix A.) Student work samples on comparable exercises, if collected systematically over time, are analogous to run charts. A psychology professor at the College of William and Mary in Virginia, for instance, has used the median performance sampling technique for many years to monitor performance on key exercises (H. Friedman, personal communication, April 25, 1988). In using this technique, he looks explicitly for what TQM practitioners would label "special causes" to account for deviations from expected patterns. Analogous to the Pareto chart, moreover, is the systematic classification of student errors—used primarily in such disciplines as math and the physical sciences. Under this technique, instructors, while grading a test or exercise, record the typical mistakes that students make and then reorder those mistakes in terms of frequency of occurrence. The potential of these techniques to change markedly both the teaching process and the obtained results is demonstrated convincingly by the success of such recent efforts as the New Jersey Algebra Project (Pine, 1988).

Unfortunately, integrated efforts such as these are extremely rare, and given the emphasis on individual experiment and decentralization inherent in classroom research, they are likely to remain so. For despite their admirable resemblance to TQM's techniques at the lowest level, classroom research lacks an equivalent infrastructure to support wider institutional improvement. Particularly missing are attempts to monitor cross-course connections and the use of common tools across a range of similar courses.

Both these situations would violate the presumption of individual faculty sovereignty that classroom research practice, for all its value, has so far left untouched.

This last observation highlights the fact that without an overarching philosophy of improvement, assessment remains an uncertain mechanism for change. Partly this is because the wider implications for practice of the trends noted here remain largely unsupported. As the first trend has shown, both outcomes and process information are needed, particularly at the level of curricular managers who must make decisions constantly about where and how to intervene, but information of this kind also requires a systematic data base, consciously designed for the purpose and actively managed by information professionals as an institutional resource. As the second trend implies, we greatly need outcomes information that matches the actual contexts and settings in which learning takes place. Naturalistic assessment to some degree fulfills this requirement, but techniques such as portfolio analysis have proved both costly and time consuming when implemented on too broad a scale or for too many purposes. As for the third trend, classroom-level monitoring tools are indispensable for continuous improvement, and we are discovering their feasibility and benefits across a wide range of institutional settings. But we rarely support systematic faculty training, and their use of classroom monitoring tools is by definition noncumulative with respect to curricular issues. Clearly, these tools are useful for improving individual classrooms, but they are unlikely in themselves to improve joint products significantly. As in the case of TQM in industry, without significant increases in organizational commitment, we are not likely to overcome these obstacles quickly.

The Need for Commitment

Assessment as a national movement is now approximately five years old— old enough for us to draw some lessons about what is needed to make it work as an agent of institutional change. For the most part, these lessons are not surprising. Indeed, they parallel the organizational requirements for information-based change previously documented in fields such as program evaluation and organizational studies (Shapiro, 1986; Ewell, 1989). More strikingly, they also parallel those factors identified as critical in case studies of the successful application of TQM in industry (Walton, 1986). Unfortunately, most often, we lack the required conditions in colleges and universities.

One such requirement is full commitment to the process on the part of executive-level leadership. All too often, assessment does not enjoy such commitment and is seen as an auxiliary enterprise. Partly this is a residual result of mandates: Assessment is constructed as a compliance function, much like any other form of accountability reporting. A more general lack of commitment to undergraduate teaching is partly responsible: In large numbers of institutions (including those whose primary mission is teaching), other agendas preoccupy top administration. As a result, the majority of institutions that practice assessment do not make it part of an overall, coordinated, institutional improvement strategy.

This sad condition is manifested in many ways. One is the fact that to date, most collected assessment results remain underutilized. While some classroom-level or departmental utilization will occur among interested faculty, institutional mechanisms are rarely in place to ensure regular and effective incorporation of results in decision making. Where such mechanisms are present, they are often simplistic or, indeed, directly antithetical to other important quality improvement principles. A good example is performance funding in Tennessee, where small differences in obtained scores—well outside the institutions' control and often well within the measurement-error limits of the instruments used—can cause notable differences in institutional dollar rewards (Banta, 1988). Another common manifestation is lack of integration among assessment functions, across departments, or, more significantly, between academic and student affairs. We tend to treat assessment in each area as a separate activity, and an institutional body or office rarely is responsible for integrating findings or for making broad recommendations about articulation and improvement. While excellent examples of such bridges do exist (for example, the living-learning communities currently under experiment at several institutions), they are far from widespread. Linkages are even more infrequent with critical support services such as facilities and equipment maintenance, parking, bursar and financial services, and registration or records—all of which also contribute to student success. In all too many institutions, these functions remain worlds unto themselves, and in the absence of vigorous, top-level leadership to span organizational boundaries they are likely to remain so.

A major contributing cause of the problem is simple turnover. It is no coincidence that the institutions most recognized for best practice in assessment also have stable, committed, top-level leadership. Alverno College, Kean College of New Jersey, Northeast Missouri State University, King's College, and the University of Tennessee at Knoxville all developed their successful assessment efforts over many years in a stable administrative environment. In several of these institutions, the tenure of chief executive and academic administration exceeded fifteen years. As in industry, such long tenure among chief executives is rare in American colleges and universities. But it is critical to making a long-term improvement process work.

An even greater obstacle to success is the general lack in higher education institutions of a meaningful, organized staff development function. If assessment is to fulfill its potential as a unit- and classroom-level tool for improvement, we must train faculty and line staff in its use and interpretation. More important, we must train them in the teaching techniques that research and experience have shown to be effective. Faculty development in most institutions is currently far from the standard required to make assessment locally meaningful. In most cases it is voluntary, and those who most need training are not generally those who will request it. Often those who view faculty development negatively need it the most. At best, faculty see such activities as peripheral and, at worst, remedial. Such attitudes render voluntary participation even more unlikely.

Interestingly, this situation is far from universal. In the United Kingdom, for example, all new faculty in polytechnic institutions engage in a formal process of staff development coordinated by a well-supported and visible staff training unit. Members of the staff development unit visit classes and work with instructors to improve their teaching practice on an ongoing basis. Staff training in these institutions not only benefits individual instructors but also serves as a visible reminder of the institution's commitment to continuous instructional improvement.

A final obstacle to success is perhaps the most difficult to overcome: sheer lack of perceived urgency regarding the need to change. Despite considerable rhetoric over the past decade, undergraduate instructional improvement is not a core issue at most colleges and universities. Promotion and tenure decisions remain focused largely on research at most four-year public institutions. At the same time, state funding formulas remain rooted in a cost-per-credit approach that does little beyond encouraging unplanned enrollment growth. The irony is that many—perhaps most—faculty believe in effective teaching and want to do a better job. But little in the organizational culture of most colleges and universities today supports and develops this inclination into an effective focus for change.

At a number of pioneering campuses, assessment has provided this focus and has in this sense proved far more than just a mechanism for gathering disembodied evidence about outcomes. But in a far greater number, assessment has not yet had this effect because the incentives for change are too few. In industry, TQM arose largely as a response to a real crisis of competitiveness and profitability. For better or worse, higher education feels no parallel crisis as yet—though the public and its elected officials are, I believe, becoming increasingly restless. Guided by the proven principles of TQM, assessment can help institutions to develop a mechanism for responding in advance to the challenges that many think are coming. Acting now, as the experience of industry has shown, is a far better strategy than waiting for change to be dictated by circumstances.

References

Adelman, S. I., Ewell, P. T., and Grable, J. R. "LONESTAR: Texas's Voluntary Tracking and Developmental Education Evaluation System." In T. H. Bers (ed.), *Using Student Tracking Systems Effectively*. New Directions for Community Colleges, no. 66. San Francisco: Jossey-Bass, 1989.

Association of American Colleges. *Integrity in the College Curriculum: A Report to the Academic Community.* Washington, D.C.: Association of American Colleges, 1985.

Astin, A. W. *Four Critical Years: Effects of College on Beliefs, Attitudes, and Knowledge.* San Francisco: Jossey-Bass, 1977.

Astin, A. W. *Achieving Educational Excellence: A Critical Assessment of Priorities and Practices in Higher Education.* San Francisco: Jossey-Bass, 1985.

Banta, T. W. "Assessment as an Instrument of State Funding Policy." In T. W. Banta (ed.), *Implementing Outcomes Assessment: Promise and Perils.* New Directions for Institutional Research, no. 59. San Francisco: Jossey-Bass, 1988.

Banta, T. W., and Moffett, M. S. "Performance Funding in Tennessee: Stimulus for Program Improvement." In D. F. Halpern (ed.), *Student Outcomes Assessment: What Institutions Stand to Gain.* New Directions for Higher Education, no. 59. San Francisco: Jossey-Bass, 1987.

Cross, K. P. "Collaborative Classroom Assessment." Address delivered at the Fifth American Association for Higher Education Conference on Assessment in Higher Education, Washington, D.C., June 27, 1990.

Cross, K. P., and Angelo, T. A. *Classroom Assessment Techniques: A Handbook for Faculty.* Ann Arbor: National Center for Research to Improve Postsecondary Teaching and Learning, University of Michigan, 1988.

Education Commission of the States. *Transforming the State Role in Undergraduate Education: Time for a Different View.* Denver, Colo.: Education Commission of the States, 1986.

Ewell, P. T. *The Self-Regarding Institution: Information for Excellence.* Boulder, Colo.: National Center for Higher Education Management Systems, 1984.

Ewell, P. T. "Information for Decision: What's the Use?" In P. T. Ewell (ed.), *Enhancing Information Use in Decision Making.* New Directions for Institutional Research, no. 64. San Francisco: Jossey-Bass, 1989.

Ewell, P. T. *Assessment and the "New Accountability": A Challenge for Higher Education's Leadership.* Denver, Colo.: Education Commission of the States, 1990.

Ewell, P. T., Finney, J. E., and Lenth, C. "Filling in the Mosaic: The Emerging Pattern of State-Based Assessment." *AAHE Bulletin,* 1990, 42 (8), 3–7.

Ewell, P. T., and Lisensky, R. P. *Assessing Institutional Effectiveness: Redirecting the Self-Study Process.* Washington, D.C.: Consortium for the Advancement of Private Higher Education, 1988.

Farmer, D. W. *Enhancing Student Learning: Emphasizing Essential Student Competencies in Academic Programs.* Wilkes-Barre, Penn.: King's College, 1988.

Gamson, Z. F., and Poulsen, S. J. "Inventories of Good Practice: The Next Step for the Seven Principles for Good Practice in Undergraduate Education." *AAHE Bulletin,* 1989, 42 (9), 7–8.

Guba, E. G., and Lincoln, Y. S. *Effective Evaluation: Improving the Usefulness of Evaluation Results Through Responsive and Naturalistic Approaches.* San Francisco: Jossey-Bass, 1981.

Light, R. J. *The Harvard Assessment Seminars: Explorations with Students and Faculty About Teaching, Learning, and Student Life.* Cambridge, Mass.: Harvard Graduate School of Education and Kennedy School of Government, 1990.

Mentkowski, M., and Doherty, A. *Careering After College: Establishing the Validity of Abilities Learned in College for Later Careering and Performance.* Milwaukee, Wisc.: Alverno Publications, 1984.

National Governors' Association. *Time for Results: The Governors' 1991 Report on Education.* Washington, D.C.: National Governors' Association, 1986.

National Institute of Education, Study Group on the Conditions of Excellence in American Higher Education. *Involvement in Learning: Realizing the Potential of American Higher Education.* Washington, D.C.: U.S. Government Printing Office, 1984.

Pace, C. R. *Measuring the Quality of College Student Experiences.* Los Angeles: Higher Education Research Institute, University of California at Los Angeles, 1984.

Pine, C. "Student Preparedness in Math: An Interview with Charles Pine." *AAHE Bulletin,* 1988, *41* (1), 3-6.

Ratcliffe, J. L., and Associates. *Determining the Effect of Different Coursework Patterns on the General Learned Abilities of College Students.* Working Paper OR 90-524. Ames: Research Institute for Studies in Education at Iowa State University and University Park Center for the Study of Higher Education at Pennsylvania State University, 1990.

Shapiro, J. Z. "Evaluation Research and Educational Decision Making." In J. C. Smart (ed.), *Higher Education: Handbook of Theory and Research.* Vol. II. New York: Agathon, 1986.

Terenzini, P. T., and Pascarella, E. T. "Voluntary Freshman Attrition and Patterns of Social and Academic Integration in a University: A Test of a Conceptual Model." *Research in Higher Education,* 1977, *6* (1), 25-43.

U.S. Department of Education, National Commission on Excellence in Education. *A Nation at Risk: The Imperative for Educational Reform.* Washington, D.C.: U.S. Government Printing Office, 1983.

Walton, M. *The Deming Management Method.* New York: Putnam, 1986.

Zemsky, R. *Structure and Coherence: Measuring the Undergraduate Curriculum.* Philadelphia: Institute for Research on Higher Education, University of Pennsylvania, 1989.

Peter T. Ewell is senior associate with the National Center for Higher Education Management Systems.

*If and when colleges and universities adopt the principles of Total
Quality Management, they must make significant changes in order
to implement them.*

Overcoming Barriers to Total Quality
Management in Colleges and Universities

Robert S. Winter

Many business institutions in the United States are using the principles of
Total Quality Management (TQM) with positive results. The need to become
competitive and furnish products and services that satisfy customers moti-
vates their actions.

Many school districts in the United States are currently considering
and implementing similar policies. Described as "restructuring," "school-
based management," "teacher empowerment," and "shared decision making," these new concepts of school management involve teachers as critical
actors in problem solving. Although it is too early to assess the real impact
of these types of reforms, many hope that increased involvement of teachers will markedly improve the quality of education.

While traditional business and school organizational structures and
behavior are changing, however, not much is heard from the higher education sector. Some applications are in place but, as a whole, no apparent
trend demonstrates a commitment to the organizational concepts discussed
in this volume. Colleges and universities remain largely unaware and perhaps even resistant to these concepts.

The real and perceived barriers to effective employee participation in
decision making in higher education may explain this reluctance. Understanding these barriers and developing appropriate responses are critical
preconditions to the implementation of TQM programs.

The Need for a Culture Change

Most training workshops dealing with TQM in the United States focus on
increased employee participation in decision making and on techniques to

identify and analyze problems and to develop and implement solutions. Unfortunately, training programs can overlook the most significant requirement for program success: the need to change the culture of an organization so that it can take full advantage of the experience and skills of its human resources. Lacking attention to culture, organizations may use problem-solving processes and techniques such as employee teams and quality circles as a cure-all. The true foundation for a cure is an organizational philosophy and commitment that ensure a continued, consistent effort toward the improvement of quality.

Deming's (1986) list of fourteen principles delineate a philosophy for an effective, customer-focused, and quality-oriented organization. These principles, the backbone of the search for quality, fall into three broad categories:

1. *Philosophy and mission*—This category includes principles that stress focusing on customer needs in a never-ending search for quality.

2. *Organizational environment*—These principles establish norms and values that dictate the treatment of each individual in the organization.

3. *Process*—This category stresses the need for problem prevention throughout the process rather than the identification of failures at the end of the process.

The fourteen points describe an organizational life-style that differs from traditional practices. For example, many organizations traditionally tend to rely on a hierarchical structure in the belief that those at the top know best what the organization and its internal and external clients need. This structure dictates the internal organizational climate as well as the relationship between the organization and its customers. It is antithetical to the fourteen points.

Although customer focus and process changes are critical to improve quality, real and significant change can only occur if organizations change their culture by modifying their human resource policies and practices. Organizations need constancy of purpose reflected through stability in top management. They need commitment to individuals as demonstrated by an organizational environment that drives out fear, breaks down barriers between departments, and reinforces pride of workmanship (Gitlow and Gitlow, 1987).

Concepts that encourage employee involvement are not new. Fine and Bridge (1987) contrasted Deming's TQM philosophy with McGregor's (1960) Theory Y, which encourages employee participation, and they found a significant congruence of ideas. Both approaches assume that self-actualization of individuals and organizational efficiency are not in conflict with one another.

Barriers in Business and School Districts

This section discusses the organizational barriers that businesses and school districts face in restructuring their organizations to implement TQM.

It lays the groundwork for the next two sections, which look at barriers in universities and colleges.

After many successful decades, U.S. corporations find that their products are no longer competitive in the global market, including the United States, even when the prices of their products are lower. Often, management blames labor for these problems, but this conclusion is unfounded. The problem lies with the organizations themselves (Sherr, 1990).

Many organizations have the following characteristics:

- An inherent assumption of conflict between management and labor, and a tension—the "us-versus-them" syndrome—that inhibits the development of shared views and purpose.
- A sense that the human factor is not a high priority in the minds and actions of top management—for example, organizations do not demonstrate loyalty toward their employees. Employees feel exploited, not respected, and they fear for their jobs.
- A focus on productivity and efficiency—that is, on increases in output at equal or reduced quality, thus risking customer dissatisfaction.
- An acceptance and reinforcement of failure and redundancy (Sherr, 1990) with a negative impact on both cost and quality.

These practices have the following impacts:

- Reinforcement of the traditional hierarchical definition of management's role and behavior
- Mutual mistrust between management and labor that inhibits frank communication and shared goals
- Employees' lack of ownership and pride in the organization and its outputs
- Repetitive and inhibiting product control systems that reinforce and justify failure.

It is in this context that roadblocks surface to changes in the structure and dynamics of the organization. First- and middle-level managers resist increased employee participation. They cite concerns about added expenditures, but their real concern is about who ultimately benefits from these changes, about the uncertainty of a new organizational environment, and about the impact on their authority (Harrington, 1987).

A survey of first-line managers performed by Klein, from the Harvard School of Business, and reported by Harrington (1987) confirmed the general apprehension of managers about employee participation: While 72 percent viewed employee participation as good for the company, only 31 percent viewed the impact as good for themselves.

Deming (1986) has identified several obstacles to the implementation of his fourteen principles. Among these is a lack of constancy of purpose, caused in large part by the increased mobility of top management. Another is the lack of top management involvement with production. This obstacle can be linked with the evolution of the identity of chief executive officers (CEOs); they have become financial entrepreneurs rather than the traditional operating officers who started at the bottom. This situation often leads to a short-term view that emphasizes quick fixes and fast returns on investment, which in turn undermine constancy of purpose. Finally, the assumption that quality is the concern of the worker on the line and that management is neither involved in nor committed to it is a major roadblock.

A review of barriers in the application of TQM in school districts finds many similarities with the experiences of the private sector. A critical issue is the necessity to restructure the roles of administrators and teachers. Sykes and Elmore (1989) state the need for a new environment that assumes that all the members of the organization act both educationally and managerially.

Teacher participation reforms produce significant changes in the lifestyle of a school. For teachers, reforms require an investment of time and the learning and application of techniques that teachers did not need when their role was limited to the teaching process. Principals, on the other hand, are threatened by teacher participation. Elsberg ("An Educator Speaks," 1990), president of the American Federation of School Administrators, describes the teacher participation movement as a power struggle having little to do with the quality of education and stresses that successful schools require strong leadership from principals. Elsberg believes that teacher empowerment is aimed at removing the power of administrators.

Chubb and Moe (1990) discuss the ever-growing bureaucracy that overcontrols, regulates, and formalizes operations and thus removes local autonomy. This condition apparently exists because top managers, to control their organization better, resort to bureaucratic rules and processes. The authors state that it is unfortunate that professionals (that is, teachers) are normally denied the opportunity to act as professionals beyond a limited scope.

The Organizational Structure of Colleges and Universities

Colleges and universities have unique organizational characteristics. They have three overlapping spheres of influence: external forces such as government, funding agencies, and the community; the administrative sector; and the academic sector. They have a dual authority system—administration and faculty—with traditionally delineated areas of responsibility that often lead to a conflict of authority (Bensimon, Neumann, and Birnbaum, 1989).

Even though administrators and faculty have a shared mission, their view of the organization is quite different. While faculty activities directly impact the educational outputs of the institution, administrators comprise the infrastructure that supports these educational activities. Faculty view administration as an unfortunate necessity for dealing with external forces and usually feel that administrators hold too much power and often interfere with the educational process. Administrators feel, on the other hand, that faculty are not equipped to deal with the complexity and discipline of administration, which is essential to the survival of the institution.

Keller's (1983) analysis of the academic organization, perhaps reflecting structures in the private sector, suggests that academic organizations should have single leadership that is "authorized to initiate, plan, decide, manage, monitor, and punish its members" (p. 35). This does not appear to be viable for both the administrative and the academic side of higher education. The administrative side is generally hierarchical in nature and often resembles models found in the corporate world. Although a private-sector perspective might view faculty as the line staff, faculty operate on a different basis than that found in the corporate world. Their structure is more democratic and participatory on matters directly affecting their primary activities: instruction, research, and public service.

Presidents must bridge these two diverse aspects—administration and academics—of college and university organizations. Changing conditions such as accountability requirements by the federal and state governments and increased reliance on foundation and gift support have a direct impact on the role definition of higher education leaders. Furthermore, to compound the management problem of higher education organizations, Keller (1983) observes that institutions are run by amateurs rather than by professional administrators. While that may be true, the job requirements of college and university CEOs are quite different from those in the private sector. Many assume campus presidents manage campus operations and serve as the institution's academic leader, but the current reality is quite different.

Derek Bok recently announced his resignation from Harvard University and explained that a major reason for his decision was the change in the nature and responsibilities of his position (McMillen, 1990). He was unwilling to endure a $2 billion development campaign. The president's job would keep him away from campus and would not permit him to be involved in the operations of the university. This is not a unique situation. Campus leaders are required to represent their institution to government, business, and community. They are ambassadors and development officers; they have little time to be active in the day-to-day operations of their institutions.

This situation affects the manner in which colleges and universities function. Bok (1986) indicates that administrators, on behalf of their pres-

idents, have become more assertive and dominant, while campus governance has perpetuated the illusion of a joint effort between administrators
and faculty. Although many presidents lack the authority and presence to
effect change in academic areas, they have delegated power to high-level
administrators on matters of resource allocation and personnel actions.

Potential Barriers in Higher Education

Barriers to the application of TQM in higher education fall into two broad
categories. Some are endemic to this type of organization and reflect tradition, culture, and infrastructure. Other barriers transcend the organization
and reflect the processes utilized to implement TQM programs.

For colleges and universities, tradition and culture significantly determine the receptiveness to and application of TQM. Perhaps the most
significant barrier to TQM in colleges and universities is that these organizations view themselves as participatory. Since they are structured both in
a hierarchical and matrix form, they assume that faculty input is present
and effective. Local governance structures such as faculty, staff, and student
senates; institutional, college, and departmental committees; and task forces
provide a panorama of inputs that appears to be participatory. Even more
significant, administrators perceive that their operating styles encourage
participation.

According to a recent survey (National Center for Research, 1990),
which sought to determine faculty and administrator perceptions of their
workplace, views on impact and power differ significantly between these
two groups. In almost every type of institution, administrators believe that
faculty have a larger influence on institutional academic policies and departmental matters than faculty believe. The survey, which was completed by
almost 4,000 full-time faculty members from 157 postsecondary institutions
and 563 administrators from 99 of those institutions, describes a significant
diversity of views on the role and impact of faculty and administrators in
the work environment.

Higher education organizations are inherently decentralized, especially
in the academic administration area. Academic policies are often left to the
discretion of faculty in academic departments, and departments even enjoy
some degree of autonomy regarding resource utilization, but decentralization is not necessarily synonymous with participatory processes. Decentralization of budget authority may not mean that the process for determining
the institutional budget allocations provides faculty and staff opportunities
to influence and guide these decisions.

The need for accountability and better management results in structures that can be hierarchical and highly centralized. External demands
have time constraints that normally preclude the time needed to reach
consensus. The situation separates, rather than merges, the administrative

and academic worlds. The academic side functions in a semiautonomous mode, providing the faculty ample opportunity to participate on academic matters, while the president and administrators take care of the rest. In this environment, faculty members often believe that there is an attempt to narrow their role in their institutions (Karol and Ginsburg, 1980) and that they are treated as employees on a production line.

Another potential barrier to the implementation of TQM relates to college and university presidents. Many presidents devote their time and energies not to their campuses but to image-building efforts that will help obtain legislative, community, and funding support. They often leave leadership and policy-making authority to other administrators, who may view the organization more narrowly. Even so, potential applications of quality concepts in the administrative areas may arise, but without the direct involvement of the institution's leader, many managers seem reluctant to initiate these efforts. Their reactions parallel those found in the private sector and school districts.

Although most colleges and universities have statements of institutional mission, these statements are not the rallying point for faculty and staff to share institutional goals and visions. Faculty members are basically individualistic and tend to limit their loyalty and commitment to their programs and academic units. Administrative staff attitudes resemble those found in the private sector. Their sense of loyalty to the institution is limited by their perception of a lack of loyalty from the top. Unfortunately, many colleges and universities replicate this feature from the private sector. When businesses lay off employees due to short-term financial problems or changes in the leadership of institutions, those remaining are "driven by fear." In July 1990, the University of Maryland announced that it would eliminate one-third of the positions in the central administration to accommodate legislatively imposed budget reductions. The vice-chancellor for policy and planning received a ninety-day notice ("U. of Maryland Will Eliminate," 1990). Whatever the circumstances, those kinds of decisions do not lead to an organizational climate that can welcome concepts such as TQM.

It is ironic that colleges and universities, whose primary function is human resource development, generally place minimal emphasis on staff development for their own employees. This undermines the expertise and effectiveness of employees, but still more important, it impacts their attitudes. This lack of attention becomes another indicator of a lack of institutional commitment to its employees.

Finally, colleges and universities have no clear understanding of who the customers, either internal or external, are. Administrators are mired in external bureaucracies that impose rule and form. These conditions limit the flexibility and creativity of the institution as a whole. Maximizing resource acquisition, improving institutional image, and minimizing criticism such as the findings in audit reports become priority concerns, rather than serving the internal and external customers of the institution.

Faculty, on the other hand, experience diverse and sometimes conflicting demands on their time and attention. They teach, they research, they serve on institutional committees, and they provide services to the community. Often, their activities and professional interests draw them away from their primary consumers, the students.

Other barriers may arise in colleges and universities due to the processes used to implement TQM, such as the formation of problem-solving employee teams:

Productivity. Recurring weekly or biweekly meetings may be considered a drain on resources because they draw employees away from a "productive" use of their time.

Training Costs. Training for team members on problem-solving techniques, normally provided by outside firms and consultants, requires an investment of time and financial resources.

Solutions. The impact of solutions is underrated when they do not translate to the "bottom line," as in the private sector.

Time Involved. Solutions may take longer to develop. Management may not have the patience to wait.

Potential Solutions

Although to some these barriers may appear insurmountable, successful efforts are taking place in higher education. Beyond those cases described in other chapters, individuals with vision are implementing TQM in their organizational areas.

What if the president is not committed to TQM? Two programs, one at Colorado State University and another at the State University of New York at Stony Brook, show that one can proceed. Both programs arose through unit-level initiatives rather than comprehensive institutional involvement with presidential commitment. Both, led by dynamic and knowledgeable individuals with active and effective teams in place, represent islands in a sea of opportunities. The success of these programs will affect the attitudes of others in their organizations, and they may evolve, in time, into a comprehensive institutional commitment to TQM. Although reliance on middle managers may raise questions on the breadth, depth, and impact of the outcomes of these TQM efforts, both in the short and long term, these cases are important models that have the potential to affect their own and other institutions.

Strategies for the implementation of TQM in higher education will most likely differ from those used in the private sector. Although organizational culture and tradition in colleges and universities will probably remain relatively unchanged, steps can be taken to provide incentives and acceler-

The task force was comprised of four faculty members from different functional areas with extensive organizational development analysis experience in public and private organizations; a fifth member provided potential follow-up management consultation as required. In constituting the task force, the university placed value on taking advantage of internal consultants. A member of the Office of Institutional Research and Planning Analysis provided consultation to the task force throughout its work. An advisory committee of academic and nonacademic administrators regularly reviewed the ongoing accomplishments of the task force during its ten-month work span.

The task force developed the organizational assessment with two goals in mind. The first was to identify where the university wanted its leadership team to be in terms of its professional development and to find out what facilitators and inhibitors to such development currently existed in the institution. In other words, this goal was to create a "vision for quality management" for the university's leadership team. The second goal was to determine where the leadership team was at present and to identify appropriate professional development activities.

The assessment used two basic approaches. The first involved developing a framework to define leadership and the value of leadership in the institution. The task force sought a framework that was concise, easy to understand and apply, credible within an institution of higher education, reflective of the complexity and multiple cultures of higher education institutions, customer-oriented, and able to identify leadership behaviors that could be taught. The task force found such a framework in Gardner's (1990) "nine tasks of leadership," which are envisioning goals, affirming values, motivating, managing, achieving workable unity, explaining, serving as a symbol, representing the group, and renewing. This framework not only met the criteria but also emphasized that both leadership and management are important in developing a commitment to TQM.

Complementing this working definition from the literature, the task force took care to gather information and perspectives on leadership from constituents at all hierarchical levels within the university community using a variety of data-gathering techniques. Constituents included those in management and supervisory positions as well as faculty and other personnel in nonsupervisory positions. The data-gathering process also increased awareness of the need for professional development.

Each technique generated different types of information on leadership. The contents of seventy-eight personal interviews defined the institutional culture, common values, professional development needs, strengths and weaknesses of management practices, and what leaders who are perceived to be successful do. Interviewees included the executive team, distinguished professors, members of the university governance structure, academic and administrative managers, perceived successful leaders, and those who had knowledge of the institutional history. The results of thirty-six focus groups further defined a profile of what followers want from leaders, the perception of how the leadership team was doing, and professional development needs. A written survey involving all managers and supervisors and a random sample of nonsupervisory personnel, including faculty, confirmed perceptions formed during the interviews and focus groups.

The task force gave a summary of findings and recommendations for action in a final report to the university. Task force members made presentations based on the final report to the executive team and then to the leadership teams of the academic and administrative functions of the university. This process served to make the final report a living document in terms of scope and recommendations.

Throughout the ten-month process, regular articles describing the progress of the task force appeared in the weekly faculty and staff newspaper. The task force sent notes to all participants in the process periodically, advising these key actors of its current activities and progress.

Lessons Learned from the Virginia Tech Experience

This study's findings are specific to one institution. However, if we view this university as a microcosm of higher education, several important lessons for Total Quality Management emerge.

Leadership Must Be a Value. The function of leadership must be valued at all levels of the organization. People must view leadership as an art that encompasses several tasks, one of which is management. Recent literature has included many debates over leadership and management. The question has become "Have we overmanaged and underled?" The results of the Virginia Tech study make the point clear: We must both lead and manage with a style consistent with Gardner's (1990) nine tasks of leadership. Although the amount of time devoted to the different tasks at different levels of leadership may vary, all the tasks are important, and all leaders must either perform them or delegate them.

Followers Must View the Management Process Positively. Members of an institution tend to judge how well it is doing by looking first at how well it is managed. Although some may view management as a negative term, the process of management is positive and is a critical variable of success. This is especially true in the search for quality, where certain management characteristics are essential—characteristics such as being decisive, having a results-oriented agenda, being able to plan comprehensively and to implement the plan, using time effectively based on stated priorities, being a rational problem solver, using appropriate ways to work with constituents, defining role and job expectations, assigning accountability, using rewards (financial and nonfinancial) effectively, and distinguishing between good and poor performance.

Strengthening Cultural Values Is a Catalyst for Change. Defining the culture of the institution provides a snapshot in time of how things are accomplished. To bring about desired change, the institution must strengthen its culture. This involves communicating a belief about the vision or direction of the institution, establishing a shared sense of values, and making a commitment to the continuing education of all personnel. The core requirement for strengthening an institutional culture is an element of trust. Trust manifests itself through such activities as delegating, decision making, facilitating creativity and risk taking, and encouraging different units of the institution to work and network together. Strengthening the culture of an institution will not occur without a conscious understanding of the present culture and a systematic plan of action. Professional development of an institutional leadership team at all levels is required. Professional development that increases the knowledge and skills in all the task areas of leadership will foster changes in an institutional culture that will support Total Quality Management.

A Leader "Walks the Talk." Clearly a leader is not a leader if he or she has not earned credibility from his or her followers. A leader establishes credibility by "walking the talk" and demonstrating daily the desired behaviors and values. All members of an institutional community look first to the top for this credibility and for a continuous commitment to quality and professional development.

Vision and Shared Values Produce a Sense of Community. A sense of community at the work unit and institutional level is critical to Total Quality Management. This sense of community requires all involved to know their roles and how their specific roles fit into the larger picture. Each individual, regardless of organizational role, must be treated with respect, dignity, and recognition for the role he or she plays in the institution. Vision and shared values are the building blocks for this sense of community. They strengthen internal communication and minimize micromanagement and fiefdom. Members of an institution cannot see themselves as partners or internal customers without a sense of community.

The Literature Accurately Depicts Preferred Leadership Attributes. Followers at all levels of the organization are able to articulate clearly the attributes desired in an ideal leader. The profile of the ideal leader at Virginia Tech mirrored the attributes identified in the literature. For example, followers first look to a leader for a sense of vision and personal integrity. Leaders can then develop the other skills and attributes sought in the ideal leader, such as nurturing, decisiveness, intervention, active listening, assertiveness, delegation, advocacy, situational leadership, appraisal and feedback, mediation, and political acumen, to name some of the ones identified. The profile of the ideal leader identifies another important area of professional development for university administrators: knowing how organizations work and having a repertoire of skills to use as appropriate.

For example, political and human relations skills are important in building networks that cross institutional boundaries. However, these skills alone will not make an administrator effective without the accompanying managerial and envisioning skills (Bennis, 1989; Kotter, 1988; Kouzes and Posner, 1987; Bensimon, Neumann, and Birnbaum, 1989; Davis, 1985; Namus, 1989; Bolman and Deal, 1988).

Managing Conflict Is Problematic. Personnel at Virginia Tech were able to identify managers they perceived as successful leaders. These leaders possessed and mirrored the attributes and skills listed in the literature except for one. The skill most problematic for the successful leaders at this institution was conflict resolution. This area was problematic for two reasons. First, dealing with conflict was not a skill the majority of the managers had been taught through any type of professional development activity. Second, the culture of the institution influences conflict resolution; at this institution, the culture included beliefs that "you should not rock the boat." Conflict resolution is singled out here because of its importance to TQM and because several other studies have found it to be a problem for managers. The ability to handle conflict is central to building a sense of community and to aligning different organizational units in the pursuit of a common goal such as quality improvements.

Differences Between the Two Houses of Academia Are More Perceived than Real. One barrier to TQM in higher education that is frequently cited is the difference between the academic and administrative sides of an institution. Although differences do exist, at Virginia Tech these differences were found to be more perceived than real for leadership development purposes. The profile of the ideal leader was the same for both sides, as were the majority of professional development needs identified.

Professional Development Programs Are Not a Panacea. Leadership development is not the answer to all the problems identified in a study such as this one. Although professional development could deal with the majority of needs identified, others required administrative review and action. For example, the study revealed the need for a resource manual for department heads. Department heads, especially new ones, wanted to have one place where they could find help in understanding the overall organization, understanding the role of different units, and identifying correctly whom to call for help with different types of problems. Such information is critical to the development of good internal customers and can only be provided through decisions taken by the administration.

A Pool of Ideas Exists That Is Rarely Tapped. Personnel at the operational level know more about needed quality improvements in day-to-day operations than line or staff managers in the hierarchy. When this knowledge remains untapped or even suppressed, it becomes a source of frustration and represents a significant cost to the institution. Learning ways to tap this resource lies at the heart of continuous improvement.

No Good Deed Goes Unpunished. The most common response in the data-gathering phase described an inverse organizational reward structure. Personnel tended to find their jobs enlarged rather than enriched. Maslow (1943), Herzberg, Mausner, and Synderman (1959), Vroom (1964), and Gardner (1990) would suggest that the function that lies at the heart of good leadership is absent in this situation. For continuous improvement to become a reality, work must be intrinsically motivating and recognition freely and openly exhibited. At most universities, no good deed goes unpunished.

University Administrators Are Not Prepared as Leaders. We believe that the majority of administrators at Virginia Tech are similar to those at other institutions in that education in the art of leadership has not been part of their professional development. It is important to remember this point as institutions seek to bring about change, especially in the area of TQM. In reality, much of TQM relates to core issues in the art of leadership. For university administrators to behave differently, the institution must provide its leadership team with the skills and knowledge they need to be effective. Administrators coming to managerial positions from many diverse disciplines must learn a new way of thinking and behaving for their new roles. A commitment to this type of leadership development was not found to be a strong component of this institution's culture nor is it likely to be in most universities.

The task force developed recommendations for professional development from the lessons learned in the organizational assessment, from specific needs identified on the written questionnaire, and from perceptions of managers about how they preferred to learn. Several of these recommendations are currently being implemented.

Professional Development Recommendations

The perceptions of how managers want to learn leadership was a critical variable in tailoring recommendations to meet this need. A difference in preferred learning formats between university managers and managers in private organizations was important. University managers, more than their counterparts in the private sector, want to learn from each other in informal settings. Building on the premise that leadership development should move from top to bottom, the task force made recommendations for programs and initiatives in three basic areas—formal programs, informal learning with peers, and administrative initiatives.

Formal Development Programs. The formal development programs focus on knowledge and skills that are specific to each level of management. These programs include the Executive Leadership Retreat, New Department Head Professional Development, Leadership Development Institute, Supervisory Development Institute, and Professional Development for

Departmental Head Secretaries and Administrative Assistants. The Leadership Development Institute, for example, which is currently in development, is an intensive three-week experience building on three levels. The first week will focus on building management and human relations skills through learning what leaders do, knowing the culture of the institution, and beginning a personal leadership assessment. In the second week, managers will refine their organizational, political, and networking skills; these skills include conflict resolution, mediating, team building, representing groups, and working with a variety of constituent groups. In the third week, managers will integrate their skills into a knowledge of how organizations work. Emphasis in this final week is on change management and problem solving.

Informal Learning Opportunities. Monthly leadership forums around the breakfast table will provide an opportunity for managers to discuss leadership challenges within the institutional culture. An administrative colloquium for managers from the academic and administrative departments, helping them learn how they can complement and add value to the total functioning of the university, will build a sense of community. A similar forum structured specifically for the deans will serve the same purpose. Each academic and administrative department will appoint a leadership development coordinator to encourage managers to learn from each other in a variety of effective, low-cost ways. Workshops on high-priority specific topics, such as stress management and conflict resolution, are planned as periodic offerings.

Universitywide Initiatives. The third area of professional development involves universitywide development initiatives. The first initiative includes an institutional administrator evaluation program structured around a professional development growth plan. The second initiative defines the scope of a needed resource manual for department heads. The third initiative requests the appointment of a steering committee on leadership excellence to provide the necessary guidance in developing, refining, and evaluating each professional development program.

The task force focused on the university's management, but its report emphasized that it is important to recognize that many individuals assume leadership in organizational governance roles. Extending professional development to individuals in all leadership roles will strengthen the commitment to total quality management.

The Road to TQM

TQM must begin with the development of the leadership team working toward a shared vision, shared values, and a repertoire of leadership skills. Change will not occur immediately either in personnel or in the institutional culture. Leadership development must be a value and a process that evolves within the institution over a period of five to ten years. Based on the work at Virginia Tech, we recommend a four-pronged approach to leadership development. First, a mind-set revolution must occur for each and every manager. Each must face change head on, beginning within. Each manager must commit to his or her own leadership development and to setting in motion the change process.

Second, the value of leadership must be demonstrated from top to bottom within the institution by every manager reading about and discussing leadership. This demonstration must begin with the executive team.

Third, every manager must have the opportunity to be exposed to and learn from success. Success stories from peers and peer institutions provide valuable lessons.

Fourth, the university must provide formal professional development opportunities. The first opportunities need to include those who are committed and who can serve as a success story for others. This four-pronged approach will build an institutional administrative team into a strong leadership team for TQM.

Postscript

By internal reallocation, Virginia Tech set aside $100,000 to fund the programs discussed here during the year following presentation of the task force report. This created a sense of excitement and anticipation among the university management group. Subsequently, the state experienced significant budgetary shortfalls, and the university was asked for various reductions by priority level. The university lost leadership development funds in these severe budget cuts. However, it is implementing many of the task force recommendations through such activities as informal reading groups, donated faculty time for development and implementation of the Leadership Development Institute, donated faculty time for seminars on specific management topics, and development of the handbook for department heads. It is anticipated that the lack of funds for the program is only a temporary delay and that in the next biennium funding will be restored.

References

Bennis, W. *On Becoming a Leader.* Reading, Mass.: Addison-Wesley, 1989.

Bensimon, E., Neumann, A., and Birnbaum, R. *Making Sense of Administrative Leadership: The "L" Word in Higher Education.* ASHE-ERIC Higher Education Report No. 2. Washington, D.C.: School of Education and Human Development, George Washington University, 1989.

Bolman, L. G., and Deal, T. G. *Modern Approaches to Understanding and Managing Organizations.* San Francisco: Jossey-Bass, 1988.

Davis, P. M. (ed.). *Leadership and Institutional Renewal.* New Directions for Higher Education, no. 49. San Francisco: Jossey-Bass, 1985.

Gardner, J. W. *On Leadership.* New York: Free Press, 1990.

Herzberg, F., Mausner, B., and Synderman, B. B. *The Motivation to Work.* New York: Wiley, 1959.

Kotter, J. P. *The Leadership Factor.* New York: Free Press, 1988.

Kouzes, J. M., and Posner, B. Z. *The Leadership Challenge.* San Francisco: Jossey-Bass, 1987.

Maslow, A. A. "A Theory of Human Motivation." *Psychological Review,* 1943, *50,* 370–396.

Namus, B. *The Leader's Edge: The Seven Keys to Leadership in a Turbulent World.* Chicago: Contemporary Books, 1989.

Vroom, V. H. *Work and Motivation.* New York: Wiley, 1964.

Linda G. Leffel is director of program development in the division of continuing education at Virginia Polytechnic Institute and State University (VPISU).

Jerald F. Robinson is professor of management in the R. B. Pamplin College of Business at VPISU.

Richard F. Harshberger is director of the management development center in the R. B. Pamplin College of Business at VPISU.

John D. Krallman is manager of consulting in the department of internal audit and management services at VPISU.

Robert B. Frary is director of the office of measurement and research services at VPISU.

As with anything new, often the greatest difficulty is getting started. What are some of the concerns and questions that can inhibit further examination of TQM?

Should Institutional Researchers and Planners Adopt TQM?

Deborah J. Teeter, G. Gregory Lozier

We believe that the preceding chapters attest to the validity of the concepts, principles, and applications of total quality management (TQM) and their appropriateness for the institutional research and planning functions. Institutional research and planning offices serve customers, apply scientific methods in systematic ways to problems, develop human resources, and think both long term and strategically. Commitment to TQM principles is a natural fit with offices concerned with processes. These principles, combined with the application of TQM tools, mean opportunities for improvement in functions, services, concepts, processes, products, and morale. Nevertheless, the issue remains as to how TQM principles can guide the ways in which institutional research and planning offices are organized and how they approach their responsibilities.

Must I Have an Institutional Commitment to Implement TQM?

Although some will argue otherwise, a comprehensive institutional commitment to TQM is desirable but not a prerequisite. Just as with other planning processes, commitment and involvement at the top will enrich the process for the entire organization, but the lack of commitment does not preclude an organizational subunit from implementing planning or TQM within its own sphere of influence.

Just as successful planning efforts may spur broader interest in planning, successful applications of TQM can be effective in developing a wider interest in and support for TQM. But the more pressing necessary commitment is personal, and it begins with a desire to learn more about TQM.

New Directions for Institutional Research, no. 71, Fall 1991 ©Jossey-Bass Inc., Publishers

How Can I Learn More?

While the business literature on TQM is already vast, the good news is that there is also an emerging literature on TQM in higher education and public-sector organizations. To facilitate further exploration, Appendix B provides a bibliography of TQM readings. By no means is this bibliography exhaustive, but it does reference materials on the quality movement and TQM tools and techniques.

Similarly, TQM seminars and workshops are presented by many organizations, including the American Society for Quality Control and Goal/QPC (information on both of these organizations is in Appendix B). Such workshops effectively introduce TQM concepts, provide hands-on applications of the tools of quality measurement, and introduce you to others who are involved with TQM. While we cannot attest to the content or quality of these educational opportunities, interest in such experiences is growing based on the promotional materials for workshops and seminars that we receive periodically.

Other networks both for individuals interested in TQM and for institutions practicing TQM are also emerging. A partial list of institutions practicing TQM is included in Appendix C, but we suspect this limited list belies the full extent to which colleges and universities are investigating TQM.

How Do I Get Started?

The most important part of getting started is to do something! Let TQM be your guide: Be systematic and scientific in your approach; in other words, practice the plan-do-check-act cycle described in this volume. Effective change requires careful planning, implementing the change on a trial basis, checking the results, and acting on those results, either by further implementing the change or by initiating a new plan-do-check-act cycle. Repetition of this cycle provides for systematic, cumulative change to improve processes incrementally. Coate, in Chapter Three, reports the results of such cumulative, incremental improvements. Too many concurrent changes will obscure the successful changes from those that do not help improve the process. By its nature, process improvement is a series of experiments not all of which will succeed.

Initial efforts to introduce TQM should tackle problems that are manageable and where success is likely. Successful changes are more likely to broaden the sphere of interest, commitment, and application of TQM.

Another approach to getting started is to develop a checklist of your customers, an immediate application of the TQM principle of customer focus. What are their wants and needs, and are they being satisfied? Learn to differentiate between what your customers claim to want and what their needs really are. Distinguishing needs from wants is not a new task for institutional researchers and planners, but it becomes essential when satisfying customers is a guiding organization principle. As you serve your customers better, it is also important to become a better customer to those who serve you. The dual role of institutional researchers as both supplier and customer is reflected in our brokering position in information systems development and data reporting.

Where Do I Apply the Tools of TQM?

An understanding of TQM principles and a familiarity with TQM's seven basic tools (see Appendix A) suggest multiple ways in which to start. Modeling such processes as program evaluation, enrollment projections, and workload analyses with flowcharts, for example, provides a systematic examination of the steps and human resources involved in each process. You can use the flowchart to assess whether there is unnecessary complexity in the process. Do some steps add costs but not value? Can rework and scrap in the process be eliminated? Most processes contain the data needed for their own improvements according to George Box, University of Wisconsin statistician (personal communication). Other TQM tools, such as Pareto charts and histograms, provide simple but effective models for displaying and analyzing data produced by the process.

A cause-and-effect (fishbone) chart is another tool for problem identification and problem analysis. The fishbone chart encourages identification of the methods, equipment, materials, and human resources, as appropriate to a particular issue, that contribute to the current status of the process without making judgments about the magnitude of any one cause. Figure 1 in Chapter Two demonstrates this tool.

Further analysis of individual causes by collecting more data on a particular process and using additional TQM tools provides direction to incremental changes that will result in improvements. Examples of problems that might be examined beginning with a fishbone chart include declining proportion of accepted offers of admission, high clerical turnover, low fall-to-spring minority retention rates, or low alumni association membership of recent graduates.

What Are the Benefits?

The benefits of TQM for institutional researchers and planners and their institutions include fewer hassles, more time to plan and think, and more resources to do other good things. Furthermore, TQM provides a conceptual framework for approaching problems that can improve decision making through the use of easily understood methods and tools.

For example, the institution may presume that the number of dropped courses is excessive. Which of the multiple possible causes are most prevalent, which of these are student generated, and which are institutionally generated? In turn, which of these causes result from inadequate management processes and can be effectively and systematically improved or eliminated? Ultimately, reduction in the number of dropped courses benefits the institution by reducing staff and system costs and benefits faculty by stabilizing course enrollments sooner, but it may disadvantage students by reducing opportunities for course shopping.

This type of management problem begs to be solved through the collection of data about various aspects of the process so that decisions are based on information, not on irrelevant opinions. Ewell addresses such measurement issues in Chapter Four.

Furthermore, assembling a team of the right people to address this kind of problem enhances the likelihood that the best solution will surface and be implemented and that the process will be improved. The team should include those who operate the process, a customer or two, those empowered to make the recommended changes, and those with technical expertise to educate and facilitate the team, as well as provide the needed data. The latter role is one to which institutional researchers and planners may be well suited.

Just as the institution benefits from using TQM to improve processes, so can institutional research and planning offices benefit from the application of the principles. For example, by identifying customers and meeting their needs more explicitly, institutional researchers can refine their tasks and priorities and eliminate projects that may no longer be required but are continued out of habit.

What Are the Barriers?

Those who wish to apply TQM principles may encounter administrators and executives who claim not to have time for a systematic, incremental approach to change. Such individuals often operate under the rubric that problems need to be fixed now (or, too often, never). Sherr, in his workshops and other presentations on TQM, argues that there is no such thing as an academic crisis and that while an overheated situation may require actions to cool it down, long-term solutions should always be developed using TQM principles. When a child's temperature hits 104 degrees, one immediately takes steps to cool the child down and then seeks to address the cause of the fever.

Individuals who, once informed about such TQM principles as quality improvement, customer focus, and systematic assessment, claim that they are already practicing TQM principles when in reality they are not represent another stumbling block. Since the face validity of the principles is hard to deny, who wants to admit to not following them? These individuals may resist further training in TQM.

Finally, institutional researchers and planners who are highly trained in statistical and analytical tools may fail to appreciate the power contained in the simplicity and understandability of the TQM tools. It may take extra self-discipline to retrain oneself to use the simple—rather than the more sophisticated—tools when the simple ones serve the purpose better.

What Are the Pitfalls?

Pitfalls are probably much greater for an entire institution that announces the adoption of TQM principles and tools and fails to implement them successfully than for an individual office that tries and fails. Institutional failure, because of unfulfilled expectations, is most likely to result in low morale or increased skepticism about the ability of key administrators to manage the institution. The downside for an office implementing TQM, on the other hand, might be that improvements go unnoticed or are unappreciated by higher-level administrators. Maintaining momentum in the absence of support may be difficult, but this is a small price to pay for potentially improved processes and results, resource reallocation and reduced costs, and higher staff morale.

How Can Institutional Researchers and Planners Help Implement TQM?

Practice the Principles. Institutional researchers and planners should serve as role models. The old cliché that "action speaks louder than words" holds true: Seeing TQM in action in the institutional research office can help convince skeptics of the merits of this approach. Once TQM principles are ingrained in the minds of institutional researchers and planners, behavior follows accordingly. Both old and new projects will be enhanced by establishing TQM as a standard operating procedure.

Teach the Tools. The TQM practitioner must seek opportunities to teach the TQM tools to others. Institutional research offices that rely on data from others might pursue joint ventures with their suppliers to improve data management. For example, use the tools to detect problem areas and determine where the greatest payoff may occur in improving a system or process. Developing flowcharts of processes can help direct action to problems and eliminate complaints about "system" shortcomings.

Consult with Converts. As others in your institution become interested in TQM, be ready to assist them in applying the concepts. Even if your experience is limited, seize the opportunity to explore jointly how TQM can improve the efficiency and effectiveness of institutional operations. TQM is not a textbook solution to problems but rather a set of principles and tools by which to operate. Most important, help others do something to overcome their reluctance to act.

A word of caution is in order here: When institutional researchers teach the tools and consult with converts, they should remember that those closest to the issue, problem, or process must themselves use the tools in order to find a solution. For example, if telecommunications has problems with processing work orders in a timely manner, you can suggest flow-charting the process, but you should not do it for them. Describe how to use Pareto charts and suggest where data might be collected so that those involved can determine on which problem areas to focus. For TQM to offer its full benefits, the right people—those who do the work—must be involved as participants, not observers.

Challenge the Culture. The fact that "old habits die hard" may inhibit the adoption of TQM. While questioning the management of your institution—even if the questions are diplomatic and tactful—may be unwelcome, successful applications of TQM to processes in which you are involved will be harder to deny. Promote teamwork within your sphere of influence. Recognize and act on the principle that those closest to a problem are critical to solving that problem. It is essential to create an environment in which employees have a stake in and participate in the management of an organization if the full benefits of TQM are to be realized. Institutional researchers and planners can play a role in fostering this environment by exciting others about TQM, exploring with others the possibilities of TQM, clarifying the principles through applications of TQM, and crystallizing the benefits through action.

Conclusion

The November–December 1990 issue of *Change* was dedicated to "Learning the Lessons of Cost Containment—A New Imperative for Higher Education?" In his editorial, Levine (1990) states that higher education is at a crossroads; spiraling costs, doubts about quality, and eroding public confidence mean that "higher education cannot continue as it is" (p. 4). While the issue focuses on cost containment as a response to these problems, TQM is another approach to addressing them and one that can be used to identify and improve processes that will reduce cost. It is imperative that institutions be aware of alternative management philosophies that can guide them through the 1990s.

Reference

Levine, A. "The Clock Is Ticking." *Change*, 1990, 22 (6), 4–5.

Deborah J. Teeter is director of institutional research and planning at The University of Kansas.

G. Gregory Lozier is executive director of planning and analysis at The Pennsylvania State University and is a member of the graduate faculty in higher education.

EPILOGUE

In the opening chapter of this volume we identified customer focus as a key principle in TQM theory. The importance to customers of quality improvement was demonstrated in the subsequent chapters. In Chapter Two, for example, DeCosmo, Parker, and Heverly noted that students as customers will require more and better services as the traditional student market declines, tuition prices rise, and competition among institutions for students increases. They went on to note that the successful institutions will be those in which constituents and benefactors want to invest.

Coate, in Chapter Three, also emphasizes that understanding the customer is an essential element of TQM. Oregon State uses the quality function deployment system to identify multiple customers, to analyze the correspondence between customers' needs and the characteristics of existing services, and to set university priorities according to unmet or insufficiently met services.

What we in higher education and other service industries may forget is that the service being provided is not an end in itself, but something being performed to satisfy or benefit someone else. We need to recognize that unless a benefit is received, the service performed is inadequate or perhaps unnecessary.

As we continuously reexamine TQM principles and explore questions that help to teach these principles, we derive new insights. Consider the following set of questions: How do you design a process? How well is an existing process doing? Can the process be improved? Why does the process exist? Who benefits from the process? As we worked our way through these questions, we began to consider the benefits derived from a process or service and to regard individuals not only as customers but as beneficiaries. We also have acknowledged the difficulty that some members of the higher education community have particularly with thinking about students as customers. We offer for further consideration these additional questions: Who are higher education's external and internal beneficiaries? What do these beneficiaries need? How do these beneficiaries evaluate the quality of existing processes and services? We believe the concept of beneficiary facilitates the translation of TQM concepts to higher education settings. Institutional researchers, planners, and others may find it useful to embrace the concept of beneficiary as they explore ways to implement TQM at their campuses.

Lawrence A. Sherr

G. Gregory Lozier

Lawrence A. Sherr is Chancellors Club Teaching Professor and professor of business administration at The University of Kansas.

G. Gregory Lozier is executive director of planning and analysis at The Pennsylvania State University and is a member of the graduate faculty in higher education.

Appendix A: TQM Tools

The chapters in this volume frequently refer to the "seven basic tools of TQM," which include cause-and-effect diagrams, checklists, Pareto charts, control charts, flowcharts, histograms, and scatter diagrams. A complete description of all the TQM tools and their uses can be found in reference works cited in Appendix B.

Brassard's *The Memory Jogger Plus+* also describes seven management and planning tools that supplement the basic tools. These include the affinity diagram, interrelationship digraph, tree diagram, prioritization matrices, matrix diagram, process decision program chart (PDPC), and activity network diagram.

The following are brief descriptions of the seven basic tools, adapted from *The Memory Jogger Plus+*.

Cause-and-Effect Diagrams

Also known as "fishbone" diagrams, these were developed to display the relationship between some effect and its possible causes. Similar types of causes are grouped along the "backbone" to facilitate further analysis.

Checklists

Checklists are useful in the data-gathering process. They help reveal patterns in observations about particular attributes of a process.

Pareto Charts

A Pareto chart is a vertical bar graph that displays attribute data according to magnitude. Information collected from checklists is displayed to identify quickly which observations are most frequent. Obviously, this directs attention to the most prominent problems.

Control Charts

Control charts are run charts (which display data points on a graph over time) with statistical limits drawn on either side of the process average. Control charts help managers determine when processes are in control or out of control—in other words, whether or not processes are stable and predictable.

Flowcharts

Flowcharts depict the steps in a process. The type of processing (such as action, report, or decision) that occurs at each stage is represented by standard symbols. Flowcharts are useful in uncovering unnecessary duplication or inefficient processing.

Histograms

A histogram graphs measurement data and displays its distribution. The spread of the data illustrates its variability and how it is skewed—important information in analyzing processes.

Scatter Diagrams

Scatter diagrams display data points in order to study the relationship of two variables. The direction and tightness of the scatter provide clues as to the strength between the two variables.

APPENDIX B: SUGGESTIONS FOR FURTHER READING

Management Principles

Berry, T. *Managing the Total Quality Transformation.* New York: McGraw-Hill, 1991.

Based on experience at Colonial Penn Insurance and Florida Power and Light (the latter being the only U.S. winner of Japan's Deming Prize), this practical and explicit book provides a step-by-step approach to transforming an organization through Total Quality Management.

Block, P. *The Empowered Manager: Positive Political Skills at Work.* San Francisco: Jossey-Bass, 1987.

A highly readable set of ideas for the human relations side of quality improvement, this book is especially appropriate for supervisors at any level of an organization.

Bossert, J. L. *Quality Function Deployment: A Practitioner's Approach.* Milwaukee, Wisc.: American Society for Quality Control Press, 1991.

Quality function deployment (QFD) is a total quality process that provides structure to the development of new products or services and focuses primarily on customer requirements. This book is a straightforward description of how to use QFD.

Brassard, M. *The Memory Jogger Plus+: Featuring the Seven Management and Planning Tools.* Methuen, Mass.: GOAL/QPC, 1989. (Available from GOAL/QPC, 13 Branch Street, Methuen, Mass. 01844, 508-685-3900.)

This manual describes and explains how to use the "basic seven" and the "new seven" quality improvement tools, which help improve management and planning. These tools help display the dimensions of an issue, usually nonquantitatively, and make the issue more tractable. The manual is an excellent how-to guide.

Cornesky, R. A., and colleagues. *W. Edwards Deming: Improving Quality in Colleges and Universities.* Madison, Wisc.: Magna Publications, 1990.

The author, a dean at Edinboro University of Pennsylvania, provides commentary, examples, and cases related to higher education for each of Deming's fourteen points. The book is useful for stimulating ideas and is among the first to relate TQM to higher education. See also the Spanbauer book.

NEW DIRECTIONS FOR INSTITUTIONAL RESEARCH, no. 71, Fall 1991 © Jossey-Bass Inc., Publishers

Deming, W. E. *Out of the Crisis.* Cambridge: Massachusetts Institute of Technology Center for Advanced Engineering, 1986.

This is Deming's classic, which he continually improves. Read Walton or Gitlow and Gitlow first.

DePree, M. *Leadership Is an Art.* New York: Doubleday, 1989.

This book consists of reflections on leadership by the chair of Herman Miller, a quality-oriented company for sixty years.

Garvin, D. A. *Managing Quality: The Strategic and Competitive Edge.* New York: Free Press, 1988.

A Harvard business school professor writes for managers, elaborating on the history and nature of the quality concept and illustrating its impact with a comparative study from industry.

Gitlow, H. S., and Gitlow, S. J. *The Deming Guide to Quality and Competitive Position.* Englewood Cliffs, N.J.: Prentice-Hall, 1987.

This book offers a good explanation of each of Deming's fourteen points and discusses how each point fits into the overall philosophy. It also provides questions for self-examination and describes possible pitfalls during implementation. This is an excellent resource manual.

Gitlow, H. S., and Process Management International. *Planning for Quality, Productivity, and Competitive Position.* Homewood, Ill.: Dow Jones–Irwin, 1990.

A useful accompaniment to the Brassard book, this text places the seven new management tools of TQM in the context of the overall TQM concept, Deming's fourteen points, and the seven traditional TQM tools. It explains how and when to use the seven new management tools.

GOAL/QPC. *The Memory Jogger: A Pocket Guide of Tools for Continuous Improvement.* Methuen, Mass.: GOAL/QPC, 1988.

This manual describes and explains how to use a wide array of traditional tools for quality improvement—the tools that help analyze processes and generate data to define problems and solutions. The tools include flowcharting, cause-and-effect diagrams, run charts, and control charts. This is an excellent how-to guide.

Imai, M. *Kaizen: The Key to Japan's Competitive Success.* New York: Random House, 1986.

Kaizen means commitment to constant improvement of quality. The author compares Eastern and Western management and gives brief introductions to a wide array of conceptual and practical tools. This book offers a good map of the terrain and is an excellent resource manual.

Ishikawa, K. *What Is Total Quality Control? The Japanese Way.* (D. J. Lu, trans.) Englewood Cliffs, N.J.: Prentice-Hall, 1985.

This is a basic and relatively comprehensive how-to book on total quality control, which is characterized as "a thought revolution in management."

Juran, J. M. *Juran on Planning for Quality.* New York: Free Press, 1988.

A contemporary of Deming, Juran explains his breakthrough system of quality improvement.

Juran, J. M. *Juran on Leadership for Quality: An Executive Handbook.* New York: Free Press, 1989.

This is a printed version of Juran's seminar for top executives.

Miller, R. (ed.) *Applying the Deming Method to Higher Education for More Effective Human Resource Management.* Washington, D.C.: College and University Personnel Association, 1991.

Discusses the relevance of Deming's fourteen points to higher education human resource management.

Scherkenbach, W. *The Deming Route to Quality and Productivity: Road Maps and Roadblocks.* Rockville, Md.: Mercury Press/Fairchild Publications, 1986.

The author elaborates on each of Deming's fourteen points, drawing insights from his experiences at Ford Motor Company.

Scholtes, P. R., and others. *The Team Handbook: How to Improve Quality with Teams.* Madison, Wisc.: Joiner, 1988. (Available from Joiner Associates, P.O. Box 5445, Madison, Wisc. 53705, 608-238-8134.)

This book includes many useful ideas to help teams work together to make improvements.

Shook, R. L. *Turnaround: The New Ford Motor Company.* Englewood Cliffs, N.J.: Prentice-Hall, 1990.

The author tells the Ford Motor Company story from its origins through the 1980 crisis, when Ford needed a federal bailout almost as much as Chrysler did. A cornerstone of the successful turnaround was the adoption of Total Quality Management.

Spanbauer, S. J. *Quality First in Education . . . Why Not?* Appleton, Wisc.: Fox Valley Technical College Foundation, 1987.

Fox Valley Technical College (FVTC) was among the first to teach TQM in its business continuing education program and has begun to use TQM in its own management. FVTC has adapted TQM for education in its Quality First program. The book explains Quality First with illustrations from FVTC's experience and it is a companion to the Cornesky and colleagues book.

Townsend, P. L. *Commit to Quality.* New York: Wiley, 1990.

The first five years of Total Quality Management at the Paul Revere Insurance Company are described here. This is a good case history of service-industry implementation, full of application ideas. Unfortunately, there are no statistical applications.

Walton, M. *The Deming Management Method.* New York: Putnam, 1986.

An excellent first book on total quality, this book is divided into two basic parts. The first part summarizes a Deming seminar and his fourteen points from the viewpoint of a professional newspaper writer. The second part consists of nine case studies on implementation.

Statistical Reasoning

Cryer, J. D., and Miller, R. B. *Statistics for Business: Data Analysis and Modeling.* Boston: PWS-KENT Publishing, 1991.

This basic statistics textbook emphasizes analyses of processes.

Ishikawa, K. *Guide to Quality Control.* White Plains, N.Y.: Asian Productivity Organization, 1986. (Available from UNIPUB, One Water Street, White Plains, N.Y. 10601, 800-247-8519.)

This is the best-seller in the area of basic statistical approaches for quality improvement. Originally written for factory foremen in Japan, it has a much wider appeal.

Kume, H. *Statistical Methods for Quality Improvement.* Tokyo, Japan: Association for Overseas Technical Scholarship Chosakai, 1985. (Available from UNIPUB, One Water Street, White Plains, N.Y. 10601, 800-247-8519.)

This is a good book on statistical methods that are useful for manufacturing processes.

Western Electric. Statistical Quality Control Handbook. (11th printing.) Indianapolis, Ind.: Western Electric, 1985. (Send inquiries to: AT&T Technologies, Commercial Sales Clerk, Select Code 700-444, P.O. Box 19901, Indianapolis, Ind. 46219, 800-432-6600.)

This is one of the classics on statistics for manufacturing processes.

Wheeler, D., and Chambers, D. S. *Understanding Statistical Process Control.* Knoxville, Tenn.: Statistical Process Control, 1986. (Available from Statistical Process Control, 615-584-5005.)

This is probably the best book on the practical aspects of control charts. It was written for engineers with little or no statistical training.

Unless otherwise indicated, these and other books are available through the American Society for Quality Control (ASQC), 310 West Wisconsin, Milwaukee, Wisconsin 53203; telephone 800-952-6587.

The ASQC sells books and other materials to the public. It is also a membership organization with regional and national meetings and a monthly magazine, *Quality Progress*. Among numerous other activities, the ASQC cosponsors the Malcolm Baldrige National Quality Award. One free copy of the application guidelines for this award is available from the National Institute of Standards and Technology, Gaithersburg, Maryland 20899. Multiple copies can be purchased from the ASQC.

Appendix C: Total Quality Management in Twenty-Five U.S. Colleges and Universities

Oregon State University, with the assistance of Samford University and Fox Valley Technical College, identified twenty-five institutions involved in TQM in June 1990. This is not a comprehensive list but indicates higher education's growing interest in TQM.

Four-Year Institutions

Carnegie-Mellon University, Pittsburgh, Pennsylvania
Colorado State University, Fort Collins, Colorado
Columbia University, New York, New York
Florida State University, Tallahassee, Florida
Harvard University, Cambridge, Massachusetts
Illinois Institute of Technology, Chicago, Illinois
Milwaukee School of Engineering, Milwaukee, Wisconsin
Northwestern University, Evanston, Illinois
Oregon State University, Corvallis, Oregon
Pepperdine University, Malibu, California
University of Chicago, Chicago, Illinois
University of Michigan, Ann Arbor, Michigan
University of Minnesota, Minneapolis, Minnesota
University of North Carolina, Chapel Hill, North Carolina
University of Pittsburgh, Pittsburgh, Pennsylvania
University of Wisconsin, Madison, Wisconsin
University of Wyoming, Laramie, Wyoming

Two-Year Institutions

Delaware County Community College, Media, Pennsylvania
Fox Valley Technical College, Appleton, Wisconsin
Hawkeye Institute of Technology, Waterloo, Iowa
Jackson Community College, Jackson, Michigan
Lamar Community College, Lamar, Colorado
Palm Beach Community College, Lake Worth, Florida
St. Augustine Technical Center, St. Augustine, Florida

Other

North Dakota University System, Bismarck, North Dakota

INDEX

ORDERING INFORMATION

NEW DIRECTIONS FOR INSTITUTIONAL RESEARCH is a series of paperback books that provides planners and administrators in all types of academic institutions with guidelines in such areas as resource coordination, information analysis, program evaluation, and institutional management. Books in the series are published quarterly in Fall, Winter, Spring, and Summer and are available for purchase by subscription as well as by single copy.

SUBSCRIPTIONS for 1991 cost $45.00 for individuals (a savings of 20 percent over single-copy prices) and $60.00 for institutions, agencies, and libraries. Please do not send institutional checks for personal subscriptions. Standing orders are accepted.

SINGLE COPIES cost $13.95 when payment accompanies order. (California, New Jersey, New York, and Washington, D.C., residents please include appropriate sales tax.) Billed orders will be charged postage and handling.

DISCOUNTS FOR QUANTITY ORDERS are available. Please write to the address below for information.

ALL ORDERS must include either the name of an individual or an official purchase order number. Please submit your order as follows:
  Subscriptions: specify series and year subscription is to begin
  Single copies: include individual title code (such as IR1)

MAIL ALL ORDERS TO:
  Jossey-Bass Inc., Publishers
  350 Sansome Street
  San Francisco, California 94104

FOR SALES OUTSIDE OF THE UNITED STATES CONTACT:
  Maxwell Macmillan International Publishing Group
  866 Third Avenue
  New York, New York 10022